T0059287

TO _____

FROM _____

DATE _____

GET YOUR HOPES UP

90 DEVOTIONS AND TRUE STORIES FOR YOUNG WORLD CHANGERS

BY **CARLOS WHITTAKER**

ART BY **ARTHUR MOUNT**

An Imprint of Thomas Nelson

Get Your Hopes Up

© 2024 Carlos Whittaker

Tommy Nelson, PO Box 141000, Nashville, TN 37214

All rights reserved. No portion of this book may be reproduced, stored in a retrieval system, or transmitted in any form or by any means—electronic, mechanical, photocopy, recording, scanning, or other—except for brief quotations in critical reviews or articles, without the prior written permission of the publisher.

Published in Nashville, Tennessee, by Tommy Nelson. Tommy Nelson is an imprint of Thomas Nelson. Thomas Nelson is a registered trademark of HarperCollins Christian Publishing, Inc.

Published in association with The Bindery Agency, www.TheBinderyAgency.com.

Tommy Nelson titles may be purchased in bulk for educational, business, fundraising, or sales promotional use. For information, please e-mail SpecialMarkets@ThomasNelson.com.

Unless otherwise noted, Scripture quotations are taken from the Holy Bible, New Living Translation. © 1996, 2004, 2015 by Tyndale House Foundation. Used by permission of Tyndale House Ministries, Carol Stream, Illinois 60188. All rights reserved.

Scripture quotations marked ESV are taken from the ESV® Bible (The Holy Bible, English Standard Version®). Copyright © 2001 by Crossway, a publishing ministry of Good News Publishers. Used by permission. All rights reserved.

Scripture quotations marked ICB are taken from the International Children's Bible®. Copyright © 1986, 1988, 1999, 2015 by Thomas Nelson. Used by permission. All rights reserved.

Scripture quotations marked NIRV are taken from the Holy Bible, New International Reader's Version®, NIRV®. Copyright © 1995, 1996, 1998, 2014 by Biblica, Inc.® Used by permission of Zondervan. All rights reserved worldwide. www.Zondervan.com. The "NIRV" and "New International Reader's Version" are trademarks registered in the United States Patent and Trademark Office by Biblica, Inc.®

Scripture quotations marked NIV are taken from The Holy Bible, New International Version®, NIV®. Copyright © 1973, 1978, 1984, 2011 by Biblica, Inc.® Used by permission of Zondervan. All rights reserved worldwide. www.Zondervan.com. The "NIV" and "New International Version" are trademarks registered in the United States Patent and Trademark Office by Biblica, Inc.®

Scripture quotations marked NLV are taken from the New Life Version. © 1969, 2003 by Barbour Publishing, Inc.

ISBN 978-1-4002-4716-5 (audiobook)
ISBN 978-1-4002-4715-8 (eBook)
ISBN 978-1-4002-4714-1 (HC)

Written with Lauren Terrell and Whitney Bak

Illustrated by Arthur Mount

Library of Congress Control Number: 2023038033

Printed in India

24 25 26 27 28 REP 10 9 8 7 6 5 4 3 2 1

Mfr: REP / Sonipat, India / February 2024 / PO #12227028

Losiah, you are hope with skin on. I'm so proud to be your dad. Thank you for getting my hopes up. Every. Single. Day.

CONTENTS

Author's Note xii

Day 1: Limitless Hope xiv

PART I: THE POWER OF HOPE 1

Day 2: Our Unlimited God 2

Day 3: Magic or Miracle? 4

Day 4: The Journey Out of the Cave 6

Day 5: Good Stuff Worth Savoring 8

Day 6: What Do You Count On? 10

Day 7: Dark Caves 12

Day 8: A Determined Climb 14

Day 9: Do You Need to Get Out? 16

Day 10: Always Good News 18

Day 11: Peace Restored 20

Day 12: Hopeful Stories 22

Day 13: Hope Eternal 24

Day 14: Adversity Transformed 26

Day 15: A Miraculous Journey 28

Day 16: The Healing Power of Hope 30

Day 17: Sixty-Nine Days of Darkness 32

Day 18: Obstacles Overcome 34

Day 19: One Step, Then Another 36

Day 20: What's Possible? 38

PART 2: THE IMPORTANCE OF PRAYER 41

Day 21: Rescue or Resurrection?... 42

Day 22: Juicy Goodness.. 44

Day 23: Open Hands 46

Day 24: Promises, Not Problems 48

Day 25: Fear Exhaled.. 50

Day 26: Bold and Specific Prayer... 52

Day 27: Hope on Safari 54

Day 28: Complete Faith.. 56

Day 29: Power of Prayer 58

Day 30: Mild Faith to Wild Faith 60

Day 31: The Power of Community 62

Day 32: Is Worry Creeping In? 64

Day 33: Big Emotions... 66

Day 34: Our Whimsical God 68

Day 35: Hope in the Darkness 70

Day 36: Untouchable Hope... 72

PART 3: THE CALL TO SEE THE UNSEEN 75

Day 37: People Made Invisible 76

Day 38: A Fight for Fairness 78

Day 39: Who I Am 80

Day 40: Bold and Brave Allies in Action 82

Day 41: Hope Through Friendship 84

Day 42: Wild Adventures and Big Dreams............................ 86

Day 43: Hope on Wheels.. 88

Day 44: Our Awesome Gifts.. 90

Day 45: Healing for Cambodia.. 92

Day 46: Lillian's Unstoppable Hope..................................... 94

Day 47: Hearts Against Hate.. 96

Day 48: A Voice for the Environment................................... 98

Day 49: The Importance of Representation 100

Day 50: Voices of Advocacy...102

PART 4: THE WISDOM TO LEAD WITH LOVE AND GENEROSITY...105

Day 51: Tony the Turtle.. 106

Day 52: Hope for Heroic Caregivers 108

Day 53: An Extra Hour.. 110

Day 54: The Joy of Giving..112

Day 55: The Power of Seeing and Meeting Needs 114

Day 56: Hope Builders 116

Day 57: Fierce Love 118

Day 58: From Despair to Hope 120

Day 59: Loving and Generous Leadership 122

Day 60: Hope Amid Chaos..124

Day 61: Lives Revealed 126

Day 62: Slow Checkout Lanes 128

Day 63: The Power of Generosity 130

Day 64: Love from Up Close 132

Day 65: Hope at the Airport Food Court 134

Day 66: Unexpected Love 136

Day 67: MLK Jr.'s Gifted Dream 138

Day 68: Who Sees You? 140

Day 69: A Ray of Hope at the Plumas County Fair..............142

Day 70: The Little Red Wagon 144

Day 71: United Young Difference Makers 146

PART 5: THE FIGHT FOR CHANGE 149

Day 72: Unafraid Dreamers 150

Day 73: Unplugged Hope...152

Day 74: Be Brave; Be Hopeful 154

Day 75: The Hope of Black Aunties..156

Day 76: Hope for Hometowns 158

Day 77: Hope for America 160

Day 78: The Green Revolution 2.0 162

Day 79: Is the World Falling Apart? 164

Day 80: Access to Clean Water 166

Day 81: Fuel for a Brighter Future...168

Day 82: Are You a Builder or a Destroyer?.............................170

Day 83: A Kaleidoscope of Experiences 172

Day 84: A Brighter Tomorrow 174

Day 85: Splashes of Hope 176

Day 86: Little Miss Flint 178

Day 87: A Delicious Place to Live 180

Day 88: One Trillion Trees...182

Day 89: Refreshing Goals 184

Day 90: A Hopeful Countdown 186

Organizations That Bring Hope 188

About the Author and Illustrator..191

May the God of hope fill you with all joy and peace
as you trust in him, so that you may overflow
with hope by the power of the Holy Spirit.

—ROMANS 15:13 NIV

AUTHOR'S NOTE

Hola, familia! My name is Carlos. Well, Carlos Enrique Whittaker Guzman Archibold Cabbello to be exact. But you're part of my family now, and mi familia saves about fifteen syllables and just calls me 'Los.

Can you practice with me? I'm going to spell it out phonetically, and I want you to read it just like I spell it. Ready?

Carlos. Enreekeh Whittaker. Goozmahn. Archibold. Cabheyyooo! GREAT JOB!

Listen. I want to let you know how excited I am that you are reading this with me. You see, I spend most of my time talking to people like your parents about things that I think mattered to Jesus, like getting justice for people who need it and loving people who don't love you back. I also talk about how to live like Jesus lived.

I normally do this on their phones while they watch my Instagram Stories or on stages, if they come to hear me speak at an event. But you know what? I can already tell that talking to their kids—to you, my awesome amigo—is going to be way better. You are going to be my favorite, and you can go ahead and tell your parents that. I don't think they will mind.

I want to drop some wisdom that I hope will get you excited about this book: You, my friend, have lost hope in something. It could be a relationship with a friend or family member, or it could be that you've lost hope in ever making that sports team you want to be on. Maybe you have even lost a little bit of hope in God because you asked Him for something and it hasn't happened yet.

I want to let you know that if you give me ninety days, and you read through all these stories, you are going to get your hope back. Not because of anything I have said, but because I honestly believe that Jesus is *just as excited* about you reading this book as I am. And guess what? HE WANTS TO GIVE YOU HOPE!

So, my new familia:

Are you ready to get your hopes up?

I sure hope so . . .

'Cause it's game time!

CARLOS WHITTAKER

LIMITLESS HOPE

Now all glory to God, who is able, through his
mighty power at work within us, to accomplish
infinitely more than we might ask or think.

EPHESIANS 3:20

am so excited to help you unpack the mystery of one of my favorite topics: hope!

But what even *is* hope? Where does it come from? What's it for? How do we keep it or lose it?

*Hope*fully (see what I did there?), this book will help you find answers to those questions.

Let's start with the first one. What is hope?

Well, what are some things you hope for right now?

Every week, I hope that the Atlanta Falcons will win a football game. And I keep putting my hope in them even though they regularly rip my heart right out of my chest. Back in the day—when I was Lil 'Los—I hoped for things like making the soccer team or getting to sleep over at my friend's house.

But there's a problem with those hopes: They are conditional. They are limited. They are hopeful . . . until they aren't.

You have hope until . . .

. . . the Falcons lose.

. . . you don't make the team.

. . . your parents say no.

True hope—*limitless* hope—can come only from trusting God's

"mighty power." In his letter to the Ephesians, the apostle Paul wrote about God's ability to answer our little hopes in ways so huge, so limitless, that our minds can't even imagine an outcome so great.

God has always answered hopes in immense ways. From mind-blowing miracles like parting the Red Sea for Moses and the Israelites to smaller miracles like keeping a poor widow's flour and oil jars full during a famine.

God has answered my hopes in big and small ways too. Like the other day when I followed this unexplainable urge to go to Chipotle instead of Chick-fil-A like I planned, and I ran into an old friend who needed help. Or when I wanted to help a stranger raise money for a seizure alert dog and God came through with more help than I could have ever dreamed.

God can do BIG things. MIGHTY things. IMPOSSIBLE things. He uses His crazy awesome power to work in our lives. The same power that raised Jesus from the dead so we can live with God forever too. And *that* is where true hope—limitless hope—comes from.

GOD, THANK YOU FOR YOUR MIGHTY POWER

AND THAT YOU WORK IN MY LIFE IN WAYS BIGGER THAN I CAN EVEN THINK OF. HELP ME FIND MY HOPE IN YOU. AMEN.

PART 1

THE POWER OF HOPE

OUR UNLIMITED GOD

The grass withers and the flowers fade, but
the word of our God stands forever.

ISAIAH 40:8

The story of Gideon's army is one of my favorites in the Bible. At the time, the Midianites were terrorizing the Israelites. God told Gideon to gather an army to fight back. But Gideon had doubts. Didn't God know he was a nobody? Didn't God know how *huge* the Midianite army was?

Finally, Gideon gave in. He found 32,000 guys to fight. But the group was nothing compared to the Midianite army whose men were "as many as there are grains of sand on the seashore" (Judges 7:12 ICB). Again, Gideon doubted God's power.

Gideon limited God.

And God is a pretty funny dude. He told Gideon to get rid of most of the army. He dwindled Gideon's army down to *three hundred* men. And they *destroyed* the Midianites.

We all have Gideon moments. We hope for something, and we think there's only one way to get it. Maybe you want to be a singer, and you think you just have to study at this one music school. Or you want your friend to talk to you again, and you think the only way it can happen is if you act or look a certain way. Or you want your family to be whole and happy again, and you believe your parents have to get back together to make that happen.

But God's work never ends with disappointment. When we put our hope in Him, over time, we see His power at work. We become more and more like Jesus. We bring glory to God. We know God's goodness is far bigger than we can see.

But when we put our hope in one event, one outcome, we are limiting God. We are falling into the lie that God's BIG story can only fit on this one narrow path. Do you believe that God is still good even if you don't go to that school, make up with your friend, or get your parents back together?

That doesn't mean you can never doubt! Of course you will. Doubt goes hand in hand with faith. Even Jesus' disciples doubted. *A lot!* Because life is a bleak storm sometimes. And it's hard to see through the dark skies.

But God can see through the storms. He always has a way out of the darkness. And the Way's name is Jesus (John 14:6). God sent Jesus to defeat the darkness of death so we can be with Him, here on earth and forever in heaven.

Think about your hopes, dreams, and goals. Are you limiting your expectations of what God can do? Think further into the future, beyond your own rewards, and all the way to heaven. Limit God less, and He will give you limitless hope.

GOD, SHOW ME THE WAYS MY HOPES ARE LIMITING YOU.

HELP ME HOPE BIG AND TRUST IN YOUR ABILITY TO SEE THROUGH THE STORMS IN MY LIFE. AMEN.

MAGIC OR MIRACLE?

> For this is how God loved the world: He gave his
> one and only Son, so that everyone who believes
> in him will not perish but have eternal life.
>
> *JOHN 3:16*

When I was a kid, I went to church a *lot*. Sometimes I loved it. Other times I just wanted to play Nintendo. But I remember one service that I was extra pumped about.

There was going to be a *magician* performing. And I just knew that magician would be asking for volunteers. When the show began, I had a front-row seat.

Trick after trick, the magician picked volunteers, but he never picked me. Finally, the magician said, "I have one more trick. But this one is actually a miracle."

That's all I needed to hear. I was so excited that I wasn't listening as the magician carried on. When he asked if anyone wanted to come forward, I didn't wait to be called. I ran to the stage. The magician told me how proud he was of me. *What?* Then things got even weirder. Mr. Magic Man took me to an old lady who asked me to pray.

Was this part of the miracle?

"Carlos, pray these words after me," the lady said. "Dear Jesus, I invite You into my heart. I invite You to be the Lord of my life. I accept

4

You as my Lord and Savior and am grateful that You are now my King. In Jesus' name I pray, amen."

That's when I realized what was happening. I had been to enough church to know what that prayer was. It was the prayer to accept Jesus' gift of salvation. It was supposed to be a big life-changing moment. Not a magic show mix-up.

The next day, I came clean to my mom. I told her that I thought I was volunteering to perform a miracle but instead had done probably the worst sin ever: *pretend* to get saved. But my mom told me the real miracle: God still wanted to be in my life. He wasn't mad at me.

God's love and power don't ever stop or weaken. And He offers them to each of us. All you have to do to receive limitless hope is believe in the hope Jesus offers: anyone who trusts Jesus' sacrifice on the cross to pay for their wrongs will have a relationship with Him while they live on earth and a life with Him in heaven *forever*!

Limitless love. Limitless hope. Limitless life. Are you ready? If you haven't already, you can say that life-changing prayer for real, right now. Then, find an adult you trust and tell them you are ready to have a relationship with Jesus.

GOD, I BELIEVE IN YOUR POWER.

I AM READY TO PUT MY HOPE IN YOU. AMEN.

THE JOURNEY OUT OF THE CAVE

I have come as a light to shine in this dark world, so that all who put their trust in me will no longer remain in the dark.

JOHN 12:46

My friend Blaine was just a kid when his acting career started to soar, but at the same time, his life began crumbling like a churro under a pile of books. He suffered abuse and struggled under the pain, making bad choices. Blaine felt stuck, trapped, in this dark period of his life. Then one day, he heard this parable a really old philosopher named Plato liked to tell. It went something like this:

"A group of people had lived in a dark cave since they were children. They grew up there, looking at shadows on the wall. Since they didn't know any better, they thought that was all there was to life—darkness and shadows. Finally, one of them saw a bit of real light, followed it, and found their way out of the cave and into the real world!"

Now, if that were me, I would have run from that cave and never looked back. But that's not what the person in the story did. He went right back into the cave, bringing hope to his friends: "Hey! There's more to life than this cave! There's a big, bright world out there. You *can* get out of this darkness, and when you do, you won't believe how beautiful the real world is!"

This story hit teenage Blaine like a piñata full of confetti. He realized that life could be better, that there was more beyond the shadows. But he didn't just flee from that darkness. No! Like the character in Plato's story, Blaine tried to help others discover the light as well. Using his art and acting, he brought joy and laughter and meaning to life.

We all have our challenges, our own caves we must emerge from. Times when we start to panic and think, *Someone remembers the way outta here, right?!* These dark, cave-like struggles could be the result of abuse, addiction, bullying, or even the overwhelming weight of anxiety or depression. But just like the people in Plato's cave found the beauty of the real world outside, we also have hope—through the resurrection of Jesus Christ. When we find ourselves trapped in darkness, we can hold on to this living hope that goes beyond our circumstances, our failures, and our deepest struggles. Just like it says in John 12:46, this hope tells us that God has come into the darkness of this world to bring light.

And just as the man in the story brought hope back to his friends in the cave, we can bring hope to others by sharing the hope we have in Christ.

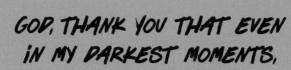

GOD, THANK YOU THAT EVEN IN MY DARKEST MOMENTS, YOU ARE THERE, READY TO GUIDE ME TOWARD HOPE. HELP ME FIND THE COURAGE TO FACE DARKNESS, KNOWING THAT YOUR LIMITLESS HOPE IS ALWAYS AVAILABLE. AMEN.

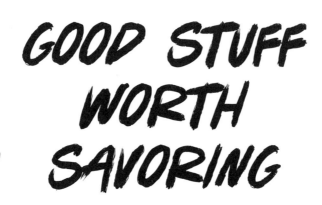

GOOD STUFF WORTH SAVORING

And now, dear brothers and sisters, one final thing.
Fix your thoughts on what is true, and honorable,
and right, and pure, and lovely, and admirable. Think
about things that are excellent and worthy of praise.

PHILIPPIANS 4:8

A while back, someone asked me, "Carlos, why do you always drink your Starbucks in an actual mug? You know you can get that stuff to go, right?" It made me stop and think, *Why* do *I do that?*

I think it started when my wife and I traveled to Italy. At gas stations, people would order their coffees and drink them right there, sipping from ceramic cups at the counter. They weren't in a hurry to take their coffee to go. They paused, sipped, and savored. Like they didn't have anywhere else to be.

I could count the number of times I had done that: zero. In America, most of us are rushing around. You'd better hurry up if you want to get to school, soccer practice, church, sleepovers, and guitar lessons all on time. How many times have you heard an adult shout, "We're going to be late!" Probably a lot more than zero.

8

But while we're busy *doing stuff*, we're missing out on the simple joys that surround us. Things like:

the sun shining on your face as you walk to the bus stop,

laughing with friends in the hallway between classes, or

the victorious feeling you get when you kick a soccer ball far across the field or strum the chords of your favorite song on the guitar.

So when I got back from Italy, I decided I was going to savor the small things in life. Things like taking a few minutes each day to enjoy my coffee from a ceramic mug in a café. And you know what? Taking this moment to slow down fills my cup (get it?) with hope and gratitude that lasts throughout the rest of my day. It also gives me more hope for all the good stuff to come.

When the apostle Paul wrote his letter to the church in Philippi, day-to-day life was a lot less hectic than it is today, but that doesn't mean it was easy. Back then, being a Christian came with the threat of imprisonment and even death. Still, Paul reminded the church to focus on the positive, the things that would bring them joy and hope.

Paul knew the very thing that I am starting to learn: that life is made up of small moments. So take a deep breath, slow down, and savor the good stuff. Embrace the beauty that surrounds you, and let even the smallest experiences fill you with hope.

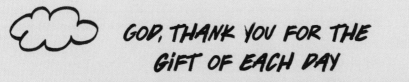

GOD, THANK YOU FOR THE GIFT OF EACH DAY

AND THE COUNTLESS BLESSINGS I HAVE IN MY LIFE. HELP ME SLOW DOWN AND SAVOR THESE THINGS THAT BRING ME JOY AND HOPE. AMEN.

WHAT DO YOU COUNT ON?

I am counting on the LORD; yes, I am counting
on him. I have put my hope in his word.

PSALM 130:5

A while back my family got our first dog. Pope was a Bernese Mountain Dog. He was the cutest puppy you've ever seen. He would snuggle in our laps . . . until he grew to his full Bernese-Mountain-Dog size of over one hundred pounds. And then he crushed our laps.

When Pope was about a year old, we moved from an apartment into a neighborhood. My wife, three kids, and I were thrilled.

When we got there, I walked next door to meet my new neighbors. I met Mike, his wife, and his kids. And then . . . I met his pet chicken. Seriously. Her name was Stella. Soon they came to my house and met my family. It was the most beautiful beginning of what I knew would be a supercool best friend–neighbor relationship.

Fast-forward six days. My daughter Seanna started blowing up my phone. When I answered, I heard her weeping. "Dad?" she said. "It's Pope."

Oh no! Was my pup hurt? "Baby, what happened to Pope?"

Through the sobs, she responded, "Nothing happened to Pope. Pope is running around the backyard with Stella hanging out of his mouth!"

Pope had killed my new best friend's chicken.

When I pulled in my driveway, I googled "What to tell your neighbor when your dog kills their chicken."

The number-one piece of advice was this: if you're sadder about the death of your neighbor's chicken than they are, they'll forgive you.

So here I was, standing at my new neighbor's door, trying to care about this chicken. But I couldn't even get *one* tear to form. So I just said, "Mike, I don't know how to tell you this, but I think Pope thought Stella was a toy, and . . . he killed Stella."

Mike stepped back. His face fell. Then my wife, Heather, walked up with *real* tears. "I'm so sorry," she said. "What can we do? Can we buy another chicken?" Immediately Mike went, "No, no, no. It's okay. It's in a dog's nature."

It worked! Heather sharing in Mike's sadness helped him respond with forgiveness. Thanks, Google!

But the thing is, I didn't need Google. If I had remembered God's command to love my neighbors well, I could have come to the same answer: in difficult times, it's important to show genuine grief, empathy, and sorrow for others' pain. We can always count on the Word of God for answers that bring hope.

GOD, THANK YOU FOR YOUR WORD.
HELP ME STAY FOCUSED ON THE HOPE
FOUND IN SCRIPTURE. AMEN.

DARK CAVES

My soul is quiet and waits for God alone. My hope comes from Him. He alone is my rock and the One Who saves me. He is my strong place. I will not be shaken.

PSALM 62:5–6 NLV

When I was a kid, I was a soccer fanático. I loved soccer. Didn't matter if I was watching it, studying it, or playing on soccer teams. My teammates and coaches were like my second family. Each game felt like going to war together. And despite my total lack of soccer greatness, I dreamed of being a soccer star one day.

Flash forward to 2018, when I heard that a soccer team of young boys had gotten trapped with their coach in the depths of a cave in Thailand. I was heartbroken. Here was a group of boys who probably dreamed of becoming the next Messi or Ronaldo just like I had. Yet what had started off as a team-building day of hiking and cave exploration turned into a nightmare when a sudden rainstorm flooded the passageways of the cave, trapping them inside.

Along with the rest of the world, I held my breath as days turned into weeks. I read headlines that shared no news. Hope faded that these kids would ever be rescued.

The teammates' families, friends, and people from all around the world gathered near the cave entrance, praying and waiting for a miracle. Rescuers and divers kept trying to find a way to reach the trapped soccer team. The boys and their coach clung to the hope that help would come.

Just when it seemed like their hope was running out, a miracle happened. Divers discovered the trapped team and came up with a plan to bring each boy and their coach to safety, one by one. As they made the dangerous journey, the hope that God had placed in their hearts kept them going.

Each boy emerged from the cave to cheers of triumph and tears of joy. The world celebrated that hope had won out over despair. Light had overcome darkness.

Though I've never been trapped in a dark cave, sometimes I feel this way. Maybe you do too. We all face moments when hope feels distant, when we're flooded by fear and doubt. Your best friend moves away. You're failing math. Your parents are fighting . . . and it seems like they'll never stop. When I'm stuck in these moments, I remember that God offers us a hope that is never ending and all powerful.

"Why am I discouraged? Why is my heart so sad? I will put my hope in God! I will praise him again—my Savior and my God!" (Psalm 42:11).

The Thai soccer team and their coach clung to hope, even in the darkest moments. They believed that rescue was possible, that help would come. And this hope kept them going, igniting their will to survive.

God is the source of true hope. In Him, we discover a hope that defies circumstances and empowers us to rise above impossible challenges.

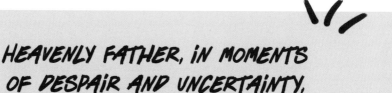

HEAVENLY FATHER, IN MOMENTS OF DESPAIR AND UNCERTAINTY, HELP ME TURN TO YOU, THE GIVER OF HOPE. AMEN.

A DETERMINED CLIMB

Let us hold firmly to the hope we claim to
have. The God who promised is faithful.

HEBREWS 10:23 NIRV

I live just west of the Appalachian Mountains, and I love to hike. Out in nature, I can take the time to slow down and notice the world around me. Smell the crisp air. But I like hikes that take a couple of hours, half a day *max*.

In 2013, twentysomething-year-old Arunima Sinha climbed to the top of Mount Everest. That hike—if you can even call it that—is known for being one of the toughest in the world. It can take *two months* to get to the top. And if that weren't enough, Arunima did it *after having one of her legs amputated*. What?! Talk about hopeful determination.

You see, Arunima had always been athletic. She was a national-level volleyball player who wanted to climb mountains and conquer the world. But one day, her dreams took an unexpected turn. She encountered a group of robbers on a train who tried to snatch her belongings . . . and ended up throwing her out of the moving train. Can you imagine the fear and pain she must have felt? It's unimaginable.

But here's the incredible part: Arunima didn't let this tragedy define her. She didn't give up on her dreams. Instead, she held on to hope.

She made up her mind to not only overcome her physical challenges but also achieve something extraordinary. Guess what? She became the first woman with an amputation to climb Mount Everest! Let me say that again for the folks in the back: she conquered the tallest mountain in the world *with a prosthetic leg*. Now that's what I call an unstoppable spirit fueled by hope!

Have you ever had a dream or a goal that seemed big and exciting until something happened that made it seem impossible? Maybe you wanted to make the basketball team, but you got sick the week of tryouts. Or perhaps you had a dream of being a great musician, but you struggled with learning to read music.

This is where hope comes in. Hope is that little voice inside you that says, "Don't give up! You can do this!" It's what keeps you going when things get tough.

Imagine how strong that little voice of hope had to be inside Arunima. She held on to her hope when many others would have given up. My prayer for you today is that you hold on to hope in the same way, no matter what you're facing.

Just like Arunima, you are capable of incredible things when you keep hoping and trusting in God's plans for your life.

GOD, HELP ME FIRMLY HOLD ON TO HOPE

IN EVERY CIRCUMSTANCE. GIVE ME STRENGTH TO OVERCOME OBSTACLES, AND INSPIRE ME TO PURSUE MY DREAMS WITH STEADY FAITH. AMEN.

DO YOU NEED TO GET OUT?

Look at the birds. They don't plant or harvest or
store food in barns, for your heavenly Father feeds
them. And aren't you far more valuable to him than
they are? . . . Why do you have so little faith?

MATTHEW 6:26, 30

Sometimes the world feels overwhelming. Chaotic. Hopeless. Sometimes I mess up and let down my family or my friends or my work. Other times I look at social media and see that a friend is angry or sick or grieving. Or I check the news and see there's been another earthquake or protest or shooting.

And I think, *God, how am I supposed to have hope in the midst of all of* this?

Jesus' disciples struggled with this same feeling. And do you know what Jesus told them to do? He told them to *get out*.

Get out of their own worries. Get out of their own hopelessness. Get out into God's big, wide world and look around at all He has made.

A couple of years ago, I started reading about bees. I quickly became fascinated by these tiny buzzing creatures. Like, did you know a honeybee worker produces only *one twelfth* of a teaspoon of honey in her lifetime? That's a lot of work for not much payoff. Yet they keep going at it.

These hardworking insects aren't worried about how much honey their sisters are making. They aren't worried about how much honey the hive produces as a whole. Each worker bee focuses on her small section of the hive.

It wasn't long after I started researching bees that I bought a few of my own. That's right—I am a proud beekeeper! Didn't see that coming, did you?

When worries weigh heavy on my back, I need to take a page from the bees' playbook. I wasn't built to carry all the concerns of the world. I can't handle knowing every single tragedy around the globe. My mind, body, and spirit start to break down when I am flooded with the daily disappointments on social media, life-altering trage-dies thousands of miles away, and everything in between—on top of my own lost hopes.

When the darkness and chaos cloud my hope, I know I need to get out. I stand in my yard. Or go on a hike. Or check on my bees. I get somewhere peaceful. Somewhere I can hear the birds chirping, see the colors of nature, and know God is still caring for His creation.

The birds have seed. The plants have water. The trees and moun-tains stand still and strong. The bees buzz cheerfully as they go off to collect nectar that will turn into the tiniest drop of honey. And I am reminded of God's power and how small my worries are compared to His goodness.

Next time the world seems like it is in self-destruct mode, get out into God's creation and see the order, the harmony, and the beauty He made.

GOD, THANK YOU FOR THE REMINDER
OF HOPE WE HAVE IN YOUR CREATION. AMEN.

ALWAYS GOOD NEWS

How beautiful on the mountains are the feet
of the messenger who brings good news,
the good news of peace and salvation, the
news that the God of Israel reigns!

ISAIAH 52:7

Have you ever found yourself doom scrolling? You know, when you keep scrolling through social media or the comments section of YouTube even though you're seeing nothing but negativity and bad news? If your answer is yes, I have some good news for you.

My friend Michelle Figueroa is a journalist with a superpower for finding the best stories. But when she started her career, she noticed a strange trend: publishers always turned down her positive stories. Was it possible that sad or bad news was the *only* thing they wanted to put out into the world? Apparently, the answer was yes. So Michelle decided to do something about it.

Michelle started the Good News Movement and began posting positive and encouraging stories on social media. A story about an eleven-year-old who saved a classmate from choking *and* saved a woman from a fire in the same day. One about garbage collectors in Turkey who opened a library with all the books they found in the trash. And another about an NFL star who took a girl to her

daddy-daughter dance after he heard her dad had recently died.

At first, she didn't have many followers, but everything changed when Tom Brady, an NFL football star, shared one of Michelle's stories. The Good News Movement took off, gaining millions of followers!

The Bible reminds us of the incredible impact that good news can have, calling it "beautiful" and something that brings "peace and salvation." And scientists say good news increases heart health and that positive stories lower anxiety.

That's why Michelle is so determined to get stories of goodness and hope to outweigh doom scrolling.

When you consume uplifting stories, it changes your perspective. You remember that the world is a beautiful place filled with beautiful humans doing beautiful things. And you start to believe that you, too, can do beautiful things.

That's the power of good news, my friends. It brings peace and hope, and it reminds us that our God is good. So keep your eyes and ears open for good news, and share it with others.

GOD, THANK YOU FOR REMINDING ME

THAT THERE IS ALWAYS GOODNESS IN THE WORLD. HELP ME SEEK OUT STORIES THAT INSPIRE AND UPLIFT MY SPIRIT AND PROVIDE HOPE TO OTHERS. AMEN.

PEACE RESTORED

When I bring you back, people will say, "This former wasteland is now like the Garden of Eden! The abandoned and ruined cities now have strong walls and are filled with people!"

EZEKIEL 36:35

Let's rewind time to a dark chapter in history: the end of World War II. The year was 1945, and two Japanese cities—Hiroshima and Nagasaki—were hit with atomic bombs. Buildings were destroyed. More than one hundred thousand people were killed. Families were ripped apart. The bombs themselves—"Little Boy" and "Fat Man"— may have had funny names, but the destruction they caused was beyond devastating.

Here's where things get crazy inspiring: Even though it seemed as though their cities had been turned into wastelands, the Japanese people refused to give in to despair. They clung to something power- ful: hope. They believed that they could rebuild their cities. And guess what? They did it! But they also did so much more.

The bomb survivors—known as *hibakusha*—have dedicated their lives to creating peace in the world. Many were only children when they saw the blinding white light of the bomb and felt the heat from the explosion. Some of them had to seek shelter at school. Others were saved by their parents' quick thinking. Yet they have dared to hope that by sharing their stories, they will keep history from repeating itself.

Today, visitors to these two cities see cherry blossom trees lining the sidewalks. They smell the aroma of freshly cooked *okonomiyaki*, a kind of savory pancake with delicious toppings, wafting from street food stalls. They can also visit Hiroshima's Peace Memorial Park and the Nagasaki Peace Park. And they can hear the stories of hibakusha and their hope to inspire a more peaceful future.

You see, when we believe in something greater than ourselves, we can overcome any obstacle and even change the world for the better. And this unstoppable hope is available to every one of us because it comes from the One who created the entire universe, our faithful amigo, God.

So, my friends, when you face tough times or feel like giving up, remember this: You have the power of God's hope within you. You can rise above any challenge, rebuild something beautiful, and restore peace to your heart and soul. It may be that one of your friendships needs mending, or that your dream to become a Broadway star seemed shattered when you didn't get the lead in the school musical. But guess what? God's hope is right there with you, ready to help you rebuild.

Hope is your secret weapon. Embrace it, share it, and let it guide you as you make this world a brighter place. Keep shining your light, and never stop believing in the power of hope!

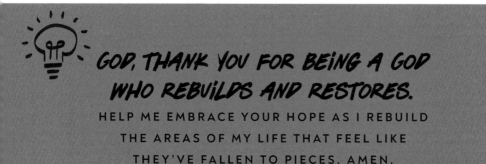

GOD, THANK YOU FOR BEING A GOD WHO REBUILDS AND RESTORES.
HELP ME EMBRACE YOUR HOPE AS I REBUILD THE AREAS OF MY LIFE THAT FEEL LIKE THEY'VE FALLEN TO PIECES. AMEN.

HOPEFUL STORIES

Why am I discouraged? Why is my heart so sad? I will put my hope in God! I will praise him again—my Savior and my God!

PSALM 42:11

I'm not a runner . . . but I do run for exercise. And to get through the *many* drops of sweat and the feeling that my lungs are about to explode, I use this running app on my phone. It acts as my personal cheerleader, saying things like "I'm so proud of you!" and "You are a great runner!" And you know what? That encouragement helps me keep going, even when I want to quit.

We all need encouragement and hope in our lives—especially during those times when it feels like we're running uphill with no end in sight. Thankfully, when we hear stories of hope from others, it's like having that coach's voice in our hearts, pushing us forward.

I recently asked my Instagram followers to share their stories of hope with me. And you know what happened? My inbox was flooded with seven whole hours of incredible stories.

Gloria had just finished her last round of chemo for ovarian cancer. Shandra was about to have her first baby after losing twins to miscarriage. Alec was celebrating ten years of overcoming his

22

addiction to alcohol. And I was reminded that hope is alive and well, and it's all around us.

In Psalm 42:11, the writer is asking some real questions: "Why am I so down? Why does my heart feel heavy?" And that's legit. We all have those moments when life gets tough and we feel like giving up. But the writer doesn't stop there. They take a turn and declare, "I'm gonna put my hope in God! I'm gonna praise Him!"

How do we do that? I've found two great ways:

1. *Remember who God is and what He has done for us.* He has given us salvation through Jesus, a perfect future in heaven, and His presence and help while we are on earth.
2. *Listen to other people's stories and find out how God has acted in their lives.* A little hope swapping is powerful. It's like having a running buddy cheering you on, telling you, "You got this! Keep going! You're doing great!"

So fam, let's make it a point to seek out and share stories of hope. Share good moments from your day at dinner with your family. Call or text a friend or family member and ask them to share a story of when God came through for them. Keep a gratitude journal so you remember the amazing things God is doing each and every day.

Let's be like that running coach in the app, cheering one another on. Because when we share our stories, we give others the strength and courage to keep going, even when they want to give up.

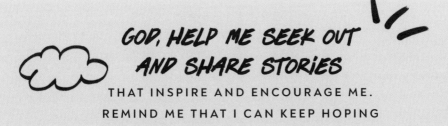

GOD, HELP ME SEEK OUT AND SHARE STORIES THAT INSPIRE AND ENCOURAGE ME. REMIND ME THAT I CAN KEEP HOPING BECAUSE YOU ARE WITH ME. AMEN.

HOPE ★ ETERNAL

> This is the message we heard from Jesus and now declare
> to you: God is light, and there is no darkness in him at all.
>
> *1 JOHN 1:5*

H ave you ever wondered why bad things happen if God is so power-ful and good? I sure have. One of those times, when I was really struggling to understand, I asked my super-wise friend Wes if he had any input.

Wes dropped some wisdom on me that day, starting off with a big truth bomb: God is all light, and there is no darkness in Him. According to the apostle John, Jesus Himself came just to show us this. God is good, through and through. There's no bad stuff in Him.

But you might be thinking, *Hold on, Carlos. If God is so good, why didn't He create a perfect world?* Well, my friends, He *did*. Genesis tells us that He created everything, and after each day, He looked at His creation and said, "This is good." When He made us, He even said, "This is *very* good." We got the "very," fam (Genesis 1:31)! But God values something super important: relationships. And for relationships to be real, there has to be choice.

Imagine if a teacher or parent told someone in your class that they *had* to be friends with you. That wouldn't feel like real friendship, would it? So God gave the first humans a choice, and unfortunately, they made a bad one. Even though God is perfectly good and there is no evil in Him, Adam and Eve wanted to know what else was out there. That's when things went downhill.

Adam and Eve broke the world when they ate the fruit and gained the knowledge of good *and* evil. And ever since, humans have been choosing pretty, tasty, and interesting things instead of God. But here's the amazing part: God is gonna wrap it all up in His goodness. When we get to the end of the story, when God makes everything perfect again, we'll have our minds blown.

But right now, we're in the middle of the story. We're living with the consequences of that choice to know evil. And here's the scoop from my amigo Wes: another one of Jesus' friends, Peter, said that God wants as many people as possible to come to know His goodness *before* He wraps it all up. In this middle part of the story, we're all part of God's plan to share His goodness with the world.

We have a chance to show others that even when bad things happen, God is good—in the beginning, in the end, and all the way through. We're living in a world where choices have consequences, where we know all kinds of evil things like cancer and war and natural disaster. But God's love is constant. God's goodness is real. He's with us every step of the way, and he's working out something beautiful.

GOD, HELP ME HOLD ON TO HOPE

AND TRUST IN YOUR PLAN, EVEN WHEN BAD THINGS HAPPEN. THANK YOU FOR BEING A GOOD AND LOVING GOD WHO IS ALWAYS CLOSE TO ME. AMEN.

ADVERSITY TRANSFORMED

O Lord, you alone are my hope. I've trusted you, O LORD, from childhood.
PSALM 71:5

One day, as soldiers patrolled the dusty streets of Iraq, they heard a strange sound. The sound of a baby's cry. It was coming from a nearby dumpster. When they peered inside, they found a helpless baby with badly deformed arms and legs. They took the child to an orphanage where he, along with another boy named Ahmed who had similarly formed arms and legs, were adopted by a loving Australian woman named Moira Kelly.

Moira's heart overflowed with love and compassion. She brought them back to Australia with her to their new home, where they had soft beds, fun toys, and healthy, delicious food. Moira found the best doctors and therapists who helped the boys grow strong and learn to walk, hold a cup, and even swim. Moira gave Emmanuel and Ahmed a new beginning.

Emmanuel's passion for music took him to the stage of Australia's *The X Factor*, where he showcased his talent as a singer. Can you imagine the courage it took to step onto that stage and share his voice with the world? Emmanuel proved that nothing can hold back a dream fueled by hope.

And Ahmed? Ahmed won multiple medals swimming for Australia in the Paralympic Games, inspiring people around the globe. He didn't let his physical challenges stop him from learning to swim and excelling in the sport. His story reminds us that hope can propel us to accomplish extraordinary things.

Both Emmanuel and Ahmed faced incredible challenges. They were born into poverty in the middle of a war, with limbs that didn't work like other people's. They were left behind. But they didn't let their past or physical limitations define them. Instead, they embraced the power of hope and determination.

These brothers teach us that hope is not about the circumstances we're born into, but about the resilience and strength that lie within us through the limitless power of our heavenly Father. Hope is about seeing a bright future for others like Moira did. It's about daring to dream big and work hard like Ahmed and Emmanuel did. It's about the faith to turn adversity into triumph, no matter the obstacles we face.

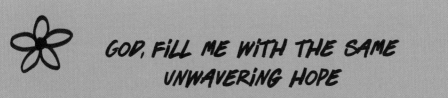

GOD, FILL ME WITH THE SAME UNWAVERING HOPE

THAT CARRIED EMMANUEL AND AHMED THROUGH THEIR CHALLENGES. HELP ME EMBRACE MY UNIQUE GIFTS AND PURSUE MY DREAMS WITH COURAGE, DETERMINATION, AND YOUR LIMITLESS HOPE. AMEN.

A MIRACULOUS JOURNEY

"For I know the plans I have for you," says the LORD. "They are plans for good and not for disaster, to give you a future and a hope."

JEREMIAH 29:11

In 2009, a plane took off from New York City. The 150 passengers on board US Airways Flight 1549 were on their way to family visits, meetings, vacations, and homes, just like the passengers on so many other flights that day. But shortly after takeoff, a flock of birds caused both engines to fail. Fear and panic gripped those everyday people as their hopes in just another day quickly disappeared.

Thankfully, Captain Chesley "Sully" Sullenberger was the pilot in the chair that day, and he refused to give in to despair. He and his crew believed that a miracle was possible.

Captain Sully decided to land the plane on the Hudson River. Miraculously, every single person on board survived! He even lived to see a movie made about his heroism, starring Tom Hanks. Can you imagine the same guy who voiced Woody in *Toy Story* acting as you in a movie?!

Amigos, I want you to think about your own lives. You've probably never been on a plane with engine damage. But we all face challenges that seem impossible. Maybe your best friend is hanging with a new group of kids lately. Maybe you wanted to make the honor roll, but you're struggling to get your grades up.

Whatever your circumstances, God wants to give you hope. And when you choose to embrace the limitless hope that comes from God, you may just find the courage you need to push through any challenge.

Hope is not some wishful thinking, like tossing a penny into a fountain and hoping for your wildest dreams to come true. No, hope is a powerful force that ignites our spirits and fuels our determination. It gives us the courage to press on, even when things seem bleak. It reminds us that God is in the miracle business, and He's not interested in being a great businessman. He's giving those things out for free.

I have felt fear. I have felt despair. I have felt hopelessness. I imagine I would have felt all three on Flight 1549. But everyone on that plane, their loved ones, and the millions of people watching the story unfold are so glad Captain Sully clung to the hope needed to keep fighting . . . and inspire a supercool movie.

Think about the power of hope in your own life. You can keep tossing pennies (I mean, it's pretty fun!), but no matter how tough things may seem, remember that hope—God's miraculous hope—has the power to carry you through.

GOD, HELP ME MAINTAIN HOPE

EVEN IN THE FACE OF CHALLENGES. GIVE ME THE
STRENGTH TO PERSEVERE AND THE COURAGE
TO TRUST IN YOUR PLANS FOR ME. AMEN.

THE HEALING POWER OF HOPE

Those who hope in the Lord will renew their strength.
They will soar on wings like eagles; they will run and
not grow weary, they will walk and not be faint.

ISAIAH 40:31 NIV

I recently met a pediatrician who knows a lot about the healing power of hope. Before she became Dr. Pratt, she was just Jen: a kid who lived in Minnesota and loved to play sports. Then one day, her knee started to hurt. No big deal. Knees tend to do that when you fall down ice skating or hit the hard gym floor during a basketball game.

But the pain got worse and worse. Turns out, it was a big deal after all. Jen had bone cancer. All her hopes and plans for the future seemed out of reach. That's when the Make-A-Wish Foundation stepped in. They told Jen that if she could stay strong through her treatment, they would grant her a wish. Jen knew just what she wanted to do. She would go to Disney World!

Over the next year, the staff at the hospital took great care of Jen and encouraged her to keep hoping that her Disney dream would come true. And it did! Finally, she won the hard battle with cancer, and she got to fly to Florida with her family. Jen met Aladdin and Jasmine and all her other favorite Disney characters.

Now, two decades later, Jen is a cancer pediatrician at the same hospital that treated her cancer. Talk about coming full circle! She's also still involved with the Make-A-Wish Foundation—an organization that grants wishes and gives kids hope in the middle of serious illnesses. And that's just as important as her medical skills. Because here's a mind-blowing fact: scientific studies have proven that hope can lead to physical healing. In a study done by the Make-A-Wish Foundation, over 90 percent of the parents and doctors asked said they had witnessed this healing firsthand. Isn't that amazing?

So fam, let's do all we can to hold on to hope. Let's believe that healing is possible, not just in our hearts but in our bodies too. Hope is a powerful force. It can guide us on our journey to healing.

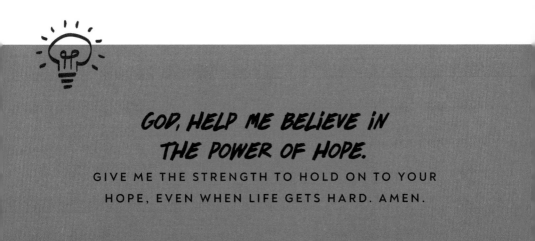

GOD, HELP ME BELIEVE IN THE POWER OF HOPE.

GIVE ME THE STRENGTH TO HOLD ON TO YOUR HOPE, EVEN WHEN LIFE GETS HARD. AMEN.

SIXTY-NINE DAYS OF DARKNESS

I look up to the mountains—does my help
come from there? My help comes from the
LORD, who made heaven and earth!

PSALM 121:1–2

Can you imagine being stuck in a dark, narrow space for over two months? In 2010, near Copiapó, Chile, thirty-three miners were just doing their jobs, going about their days, probably counting down the hours until they would be home eating empanadas (mmm, delicioso). Then suddenly, disaster struck. A massive rock collapsed, trapping them inside the mine. It was a terrifying situation, but guess what? The world refused to give up hope.

For more than two months, people from all around the globe joined together in prayer and support. They sent supplies, encouragement, and experts to help with the rescue efforts. It was like the whole world held its breath, waiting for a miracle.

And that miracle came! After sixty-nine long days, the rescuers reached the trapped miners one by one, bringing them back to the surface. The world watched as each miner emerged, saw their loved ones—people they thought they might never see again—and fell into their arms, weeping. Families and friends celebrated. The world gave a triumphant whoop!

Sometimes we are living life, doing what we're supposed to do—making the bed, taking the bus to school, eating lunch in the cafeteria, coming home and doing chores—when things fall apart. The miners were just doing their jobs when life stopped. But even when things fall apart, we always have something to hold on to: hope.

Our hope is not in ourselves or in the world. Our hope comes from the Lord, the Maker of heaven and earth. When we face tough times or feel trapped in darkness, we can lift our eyes and remember that our help comes from our good God.

The Chilean miners' rescue shows us that even in the darkest moments, God is at work. When Jesus died, it wasn't because He was doing anything wrong or God didn't have a plan. Even when his followers and everyone else thought the worst had happened, God was still at work. Jesus' death was the ultimate plan to save us! Three days later, Jesus emerged from the tomb alive. God brings people together, fuels hope, and shows us that miracles are possible.

So when you feel like life is caving in, like you're trapped in darkness, remember that God is at work. Lift your eyes to the mountains, seek His presence, and trust that He will bring you through.

GOD, HELP ME STAY CONNECTED TO YOU

AND TRUST IN YOUR PLANS, EVEN WHEN
THINGS SEEM IMPOSSIBLE. AMEN.

OBSTACLES OVERCOME

> The LORD is close to the brokenhearted; he
> rescues those whose spirits are crushed.
>
> PSALM 34:18

Nick Vujicic was born with a rare condition called tetra-amelia syndrome, which means he was born without arms and legs. Can you imagine what that must have been like? Talk about a tough challenge! But Nick didn't let that stop him. No way!

Growing up, Nick went through some dark times. As I'm sure you're aware, kids aren't always the nicest when it comes to bullying and name-calling (adults can be even worse, unfortunately). And there were years when Nick found himself feeling down and even questioning his worth. But God had big plans for this guy.

At age fifteen, Nick became a Christian and discovered that his worth wasn't defined by his appearance or abilities. It was all about his heart and the love God had for him. The more Nick learned about God, the more his hope grew too. Knowing that he serves a powerful God, Nick even keeps a pair of shoes in the back of his closet in case God decides to make his legs grow one day. Seriously!

But Nick isn't waiting around for that to happen. He is living life to the fullest now. He can swim, golf, back flip off a diving board, drive a boat—everything he could do if he had been born with arms and legs. He has also found his God-given talent as a motivational speaker. He speaks at schools, inspiring kids like you to see beyond physical limitations and believe in their own potential.

Here's the coolest part: Nick didn't even stop *there*. He took it a step further and founded an organization called Life Without Limbs. They provide support, encouragement, and hope to people facing their own challenges.

You know what, my friends? Life can get tough. We all face struggles and obstacles along the way. But let me tell you a little secret: in those moments when we feel the weakest, God is the closest to us, and His strength shines through the brightest. He can take our challenges and turn them into something beautiful.

Nick's story reminds us that even when life gets really hard, maybe especially then, God can use us to bring hope to others. We don't need to have it all figured out or be perfect. God looks at our hearts and says, "Hey, I can work with that!"

Amigos, no matter what you think is wrong with you, or what limitations you see, God can take you further than you ever thought possible. So go out there and be unstoppable! Remember, with God by your side, there's nothing you can't do.

GOD, THANK YOU FOR USING ME

TO BRING HOPE NO MATTER WHAT I FACE. HELP
ME TRUST AT ALL TIMES THAT YOU ARE WITH ME
AND HAVE INCREDIBLE PLANS FOR ME. AMEN.

ONE STEP, THEN ANOTHER

Rejoice in our confident hope. Be patient
in trouble, and keep on praying.
ROMANS 12:12

Mount Everest is the tallest peak in the world, and climbing it is the ultimate challenge, even for grown-ups. But guess what? A girl named Malavath Purna climbed Mount Everest at just *thirteen years old*! Fueled by hopeful determination, she conquered that mighty mountain.

Malavath faced some serious obstacles. She was born in India, a country with a caste system—a way of dividing people into different groups based on the family they are born into. A person's caste determines the job they can have and who they can marry. Some people have more opportunities and privileges. Because Malavath was born into the lowest, poorest caste, she had basically no opportunities or privileges.

Until age ten, Malavath lived in a village so remote that the nearest hospital was thirty-seven miles away. Then she joined a special government school, and it was there that she became interested in rock climbing and applied to be part of a government-funded expedition for students like her.

A lot of hard work lay ahead. Malavath shivered during her first rock-climbing training when another student fell and injured his head. Over the next eight months, she trained rigorously. She was sent to a mountaineering institute where she climbed mountains up to 17,000 feet high. She then went to a new location where she learned to walk on the snow and ice and survive in freezing temperatures.

Finally, she and another student, along with their guides, began their trek up Mount Everest. One step at a time, she inched closer to her goal. It took nearly two months to make it to the summit—the top—of the mountain. She avoided rocky cliffs and loose snow. Ferocious wind whipped her face and screamed in her ears.

Still, she believed that she could achieve the impossible. And she did! Not only did she make it to the top of Mount Everest, but by the time Malavath was twenty-two years old, she had also climbed the highest peak on each of the seven continents.

Have you ever had a big dream, but it felt like a million things had to change for it to come true? Maybe your Mount Everest is wanting to grow up and become a doctor, but you're struggling in science class. Or you've dreamed of flying on an airplane someday, but you don't think you can get over your fear of heights.

Scripture reminds us of the power of hope in our lives. Just like Malavath's hope led her to the summit of Mount Everest, we can trust that God's hope will guide us and inspire us as we pursue our dreams. No matter what obstacles come our way, let's hold on to our confident hope and keep on praying. With God's hope in our hearts, we can conquer the mountains in our lives.

GOD, THANK YOU FOR THE INCREDIBLE POWER OF HOPE.

HELP ME HOLD ON TO IT WHEN TROUBLE COMES MY WAY, AND GIVE ME THE STRENGTH AND COURAGE TO PURSUE MY DREAMS. AMEN.

WHAT'S POSSIBLE?

But I will keep on hoping for your help;
I will praise you more and more.

PSALM 71:14

Just like explorers hundreds of years ago set sail to discover new lands, people today are setting out to explore different planets. Specifically, the planet Mars. Why? Because even if men aren't *really* from Mars, scientists believe that it is the most likely planet besides Earth that can support human life.

So far, only unmanned rovers have explored this great red planet, but NASA scientists are planning human-led missions to Mars for the 2030s. They hope groups of brave and curious explorers can land on Mars. Once there, these astronauts would conduct experiments, study weather patterns, take soil and rock samples, make maps of the terrain, and set up livable habitats and communication with Earth.

One potential Mars explorer is Alyssa Carson. At twenty-two, she's too young to be an official NASA astronaut, but she has her sights set on traveling to Mars one day. When she was seven, she went to her first space camp in Huntsville, Alabama, and she's the only person to go to *every* NASA space camp in the world. Even the ones in Turkey and Canada!

One of the most amazing things about the Mars missions is how they showcase the endless capacity of humans to hope. Think about it—despite the challenges, the risks, and the vastness of space, we continue to dream, explore, and push the boundaries of what's possible. We hope for a better tomorrow, hope for new discoveries, and hope for the possibility of expanding our horizons beyond Earth.

Sometimes life can feel like a vast unknown too. We may face challenges, uncertainties, and moments when we're not sure what lies ahead. But in those times, we can hold on to the hope that God has amazing plans for each and every one of us, and His infinite hope lies within us.

God's hope is like a spark that ignites our hearts and fills us with a sense of wonder and possibility. When we gaze at the night sky, when we see the determination of those involved in the Mars missions, we catch a glimpse of that divine hope. It reminds us that we are part of something so much bigger than ourselves.

So, mis amigos, let us marvel at the endless capacity for hope that lives in us. Let's embrace the spirit of exploration, the spirit of dreaming big, and the spirit of never giving up. As we journey through life, let's continue to reach for the stars and believe that the future is full of possibilities.

With God's hope as our compass, there's no limit to what life can bring on this planet . . . and beyond.

GOD, THANK YOU FOR THE INCREDIBLE CAPACITY FOR HOPE YOU PUT IN ME. HELP ME ALWAYS HOLD ON TO THE HOPE OF A FUTURE FILLED WITH ENDLESS POSSIBILITIES. AMEN.

PART 2

THE IMPORTANCE OF PRAYER

RESCUE OR RESURRECTION?

It is by his great mercy that we have been born again, because God raised Jesus Christ from the dead. Now we live with great expectation.

1 PETER 1:3

I connect with God in a lot of ways: reading His Word, singing songs of worship, and hanging out with other Christians. But I have one favorite, simple, powerful way of connecting with God that's available everywhere I go. It doesn't require a Bible or Bible app or music or other people. It just requires me.

It's prayer.

Prayer is so simple. All you do is talk. To God. About all kinds of things. Still, I somehow manage to get it twisted. I forget to pray for the sake of connection, and I start to pray for the sake of *getting something* from God.

There's this powerful story in the Bible about a father asking Jesus to heal his daughter. Jairus's daughter was extremely ill. She was dying. So Jairus went in search of Jesus. "When he saw Jesus, he fell at his feet, pleading fervently with him. 'My little daughter is dying,' he said. 'Please come and lay your hands on her; heal her so she can live.' Jesus went with him" (Mark 5:22–24).

But then Jesus stopped. A woman who had been sick for many

years had touched the hem of His robe. The Bible says something really cool: "Jesus realized at once that healing power had gone out from him" (verse 30). Jesus knew the woman had been healed, but He still stopped to speak with her—to connect. At this point, Jairus must have been getting super antsy, if not downright angry. What about his daughter?

And then messengers arrived. "They told him, 'Your daughter is dead. There's no use troubling the Teacher now'" (verse 35). I can only imagine how Jairus's heart sank. He had been so hopeful that Jesus would help!

But Jesus always comes through.

"Jesus overheard them and said to Jairus, 'Don't be afraid. Just have faith'" (verse 36). Then Jesus followed Jairus home. He stood in front of that little girl's body and said, "Little girl, get up!"(verse 41). And she did!

Jairus had asked God to rescue his family. But instead of a rescue, Jesus gave Jairus a *resurrection*. And Jairus got to see who Jesus really is—the mighty God—and connect with Him.

Have you ever begged Jesus to heal a situation in your life, but that healing didn't come? It's hope crushing! Then you see somebody else get answers, and you just don't understand. Even so, don't stop. Keep hoping. Keep praying. Keep connecting.

GOD, THANK YOU FOR ALWAYS COMING THROUGH FOR ME.

WHEN I PRAY, HELP ME FOCUS MY MIND ON CONNECTING WITH YOU AND YOUR BIG STORY. AMEN.

JUICY GOODNESS

The Holy Spirit produces this kind of fruit in our lives: love, joy, peace, patience, kindness, goodness, faithfulness, gentleness, and self-control.

GALATIANS 5:22–23

Did you know that every single piece of fruit you eat comes from the center of a flower? It's true. Strawberries start as these beautiful little white flowers with bright yellow centers that grow until the petals fall away and the center fills with bright red, juicy berry goodness.

Apples come from the center of apple flowers. Pears come from the center of pear flowers. Tomatoes come from the center of tomato flowers. Yes, tomatoes are fruits. But even if they weren't, vegetables come from flowers too!

We live in a culture where everyone wants to be seen. Everyone wants to be noticed. Everyone wants to be the most beautiful flower in the bunch. But what good is being the most beautiful flower if you don't have fruit growing from inside of you?

The Bible says that God's Holy Spirit gives us some pretty sweet fruits! Wouldn't you like some love, joy, and peace for breakfast? Or some patience and kindness in your lunch box? If we fed on all that spiritual fruit every day, hope would be a lot easier to hold on to.

So how do we grow more? The same way the fruits we eat are grown—by staying connected to the plant they grow on.

Jesus told His followers: "I am the true vine" (John 15:1 NIV). He went on to say:

> Remain in me, and I will remain in you. For a branch cannot produce fruit if it is severed from the vine, and you cannot be fruitful unless you remain in me.
>
> Yes, I am the vine; you are the branches. Those who remain in me, and I in them, will produce much fruit. For apart from me you can do nothing. (verses 4–5)

How, exactly, do we remain in Him? And *how* does He remain in us? After He died and was resurrected, Jesus spent time with His followers, saying goodbye, giving instructions, explaining what in the world had just happened. Then, just before He rose into the sky in front of everyone's faces on His way to heaven, Jesus explained that He and His Father (God) would remain in their hearts through another God-person: the Holy Spirit.

And what does the Holy Spirit produce out of our hearts? That's right! The fruit of love, joy, peace, patience, kindness, goodness, faithfulness, gentleness, and self-control.

Remember what I said about the strawberries? The fruit actually comes *after* the petals—the prettiest part of the flower—have fallen off. The most important part of you isn't the beauty we all *see*. It's the sweet, juicy fruit of the Holy Spirit that grows out of your heart when you stay connected to Jesus.

JESUS, HELP ME

TO PRODUCE THE KIND OF FRUIT
THAT BRINGS HOPE TO MYSELF AND
OTHERS AROUND ME. AMEN.

OPEN HANDS

"Don't be afraid," he said. "Take courage. I am here!"

MATTHEW 14:27

A while back, I was the last person to board a plane to Atlanta. As I walked down the aisle, I realized I had become Public Enemy Number One. Everyone was praying, hoping that the seat next to them would remain empty. Then a man at the very back locked eyes with me. Game over. I asked to sit next to him. He glared at me, crossed his arms, and grunted.

So I took my place in the middle seat, expecting a long and uncomfortable flight next to the Rudest Man in America.

Fast-forward *four* hours. The plane started to bounce more than usual, and the pilot's voice crackled over the intercom, announcing that the winds were blowing forty miles an hour in Atlanta. To land safely, they needed the winds to calm down . . . *a lot*. Amigos, I'm sure more than a few palms were sweating at this point.

I looked at the Rudest Man in America, and to my surprise, he was trembling. His large hands gripped the seat in front of him with all his might. He was scared. And I knew I needed to pray for him. So I closed my eyes and silently asked God for peace and safety.

But you know what, friends? Prayer isn't just about words. It's about action too. So I took a deep breath and opened my hand closest to the man, palm up, resting it on my lap. Five cold, wet fingers interlocked with mine. I couldn't believe it—I was holding hands with

46

the Rudest Man in America. We held on tightly as the turbulence continued.

Eventually, we landed safely, and I turned to look at him. I was expecting *some* acknowledgment, but he let go of my hand, stood up, and walked off the plane without saying a word. I felt confused and maybe a bit disappointed. But God quickly reminded me that I had been used by Him to extend hope and comfort to someone who needed it.

In Matthew 14, there's a story about Jesus' disciple Peter walking out toward Him on the water. When Peter became afraid of the wind around him, he began to sink. But Jesus reached out His hand, caught Peter, and said, "O you of little faith, why did you doubt?" (verse 31 ESV).

You see, prayer and hope are traveling companions—prayer is like taking God's open hand. Just like Peter reached out his hand and was rescued by Jesus. And we can open our hearts and hands in prayer to receive the hope God offers. We can offer that hope to others, too, as the hands and feet of Jesus.

GOD, HELP ME OPEN MY HANDS AND HEART

TO RECEIVE YOUR HOPE THROUGH PRAYER.
THEN GIVE ME THE COURAGE TO EXTEND
THAT HOPE TO OTHERS. AMEN.

PROMISES, NOT PROBLEMS

**Your word is a lamp to guide my feet
and a light for my path.**
PSALM 119:105

I'm going to let you in on a secret that could help all of us better connect with God: we need to change the way we pray.

A while back, my prayers were all about my problems. I would pour out my worries, my anxieties, and my fears. "God, please keep me safe on the road today." "God, please don't let me look like a fool in front of all these people." "God, please don't let there be a spider in the garage."

And don't get me wrong: it's good to share those things with God. But I realized that I was missing out on something extraordinary. So I started praying promises instead of problems.

Let me explain what that means. Instead of just focusing on my worries, I opened up the Word of God—the Bible. I found the promises He has given us, and I started praying those promises back to Him. My prayers transformed from a list of worries to declarations of faith. And let me tell you, it made all the difference.

I would say things like "I am the body of Christ" (1 Corinthians 12:27) and "I overcome evil with good" (Romans 12:21).

Can you feel the power in those words? When we pray these

promises, we align our thoughts and desires with God's truth. We declare His goodness, His faithfulness, and His power over our lives. And it changes *everything*.

What would happen if, the next time you faced a tough situation at school or struggled with self-doubt, you prayed God's promises instead of praying only about these problems? How would it feel to declare His truth over your life when you need it most? I'm confident that you would watch God's limitless hope begin to fill your heart and transform your circumstances.

God's promises are like a treasure chest filled with endless blessings just for us:

- He promises to never leave us or forsake us (Deuteronomy 31:6).
- He promises to give us strength when we're feeling weak (Isaiah 40:29).
- He promises to guide us and show us the right path (Proverbs 3:5–6).
- He promises to comfort us in times of sadness and wipe away every tear (Revelation 21:4).
- He promises that absolutely nothing can separate us from His love (Romans 8:38–39).

That last one is my very favorite!

Aren't these promises incredible? As you pray them, allow these promises to fill your heart with hope, joy, and confidence.

GOD, THANK YOU FOR YOUR INCREDIBLE PROMISES.

HELP ME SHIFT MY PRAYERS FROM FOCUSING ON MY PROBLEMS TO DECLARING THESE HOPE-FILLED PROMISES OVER MY LIFE. AMEN.

FEAR EXHALED

Don't worry about anything; instead, pray
about everything. Tell God what you need,
and thank him for all he has done.

PHILIPPIANS 4:6

Fam, hope is my brand. It's like my *thing*. Still, there are times when I *really* struggle to find hope. During those times, I have learned to lean on prayer.

A few years ago, my seventeen-year-old daughter Sohaila was having terrible chest pain that just wouldn't go away. We thought it might be a muscle strain, but things got worse when we were on a family trip to New York City. The pain felt like a ton of bricks crushing her chest. She couldn't enjoy her favorite city with her favorite people. (I added that last part, but every seventeen-year-old thinks her parents are the greatest, right?)

We decided to cut our trip short. Back home, the doctors told us that they suspected lymphoma. That's a kind of cancer.

The C word made me shiver. I couldn't breathe. I escaped to the bathroom, looked in the mirror, and asked God for strength. And that's when prayer became my lifeline.

With trembling hands and a heavy heart, I poured out my worries, my fears, and my hopes to God. I told Him every little detail of our situation and asked for His healing touch upon my daughter. And you know what? God heard our prayers. The doctors did another scan and determined Sohaila did not have cancer after all.

But the journey wasn't over. Over the next *three weeks* in the

hospital, Sohaila had to face surgeries, painful coughing fits, and uncertainty. It was a roller-coaster ride. But you know what kept us going? Prayer. We leaned on God, knowing that He was with us every step of the way.

During those long nights filled with tears and fear, we prayed. And God, in His infinite love and mercy, helped us find a way to inhale hope and exhale fear and doubt. Prayer connected us to God's unfailing love, reminding us that we were never alone. Finally, the doctors found the right medicine to allow Sohaila to breathe deeply again.

Here's the deal, my friends: prayer is powerful. It's not just a string of words or wishful thinking. Prayer is a direct line to the One who holds the universe in His hands. When we pray, we invite God into our lives, allowing Him to work miracles, heal our hurts, and fill us with hope.

So keep praying! God hears you, and He's right there, ready to fill your heart with hope so you can breathe it back into the world.

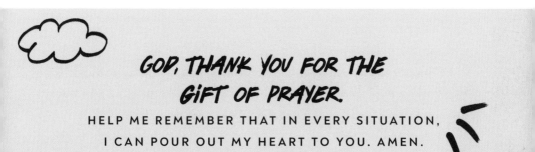

GOD, THANK YOU FOR THE GIFT OF PRAYER.

HELP ME REMEMBER THAT IN EVERY SITUATION,
I CAN POUR OUT MY HEART TO YOU. AMEN.

BOLD AND SPECIFIC PRAYER

Keep on asking, and you will receive what you ask
for. Keep on seeking, and you will find. Keep on
knocking, and the door will be opened to you.

MATTHEW 7:7

I am known around my circle of friends as the guy who hears the voice of God. Some people think it's cool. Some people avoid talking with me about the voices in my head. But I'm here to tell you that you really *can* hear the voice of God.

Don't believe me? My friend Marcus is proof. One day, I challenged him to ask God a specific question: where we should go for lunch. Marcus was scared he wouldn't hear from God. But I encouraged him to trust and believe.

So Marcus closed his eyes and prayed, "God, where do you want Carlos and me to go for lunch?" After a minute, he timidly told me, "Okay, I don't know if this was God or not, but I saw a Thai restaurant near the Titans' stadium . . ."

"Let's go," I said.

Little did we know, God had a surprise waiting for us. No, Jesus didn't show His face in the steam of our tom kha gai soup. In fact, we had a perfectly normal, uneventful lunch. And then.

As we walked to the parking lot after our meal, a person came sprinting toward Marcus. He looked shaken but determined. He said, "You might think I'm crazy, but do you sometimes work from the Frothy Monkey coffee shop? Two weeks ago, I felt a strong urge to pray for you but chickened out. Today, when I saw you in the restaurant, I couldn't let you go twice. Can I please pray for you?"

Marcus's eyes widened with astonishment. From that moment on, his prayer life was forever transformed.

Amigos, God is not limited by our doubts or fears. He longs to reveal Himself in remarkable ways. But here's the secret: if we want to receive this abundant blessing of hearing His voice, we can't limit God by praying for general, broad things. If Marcus had just prayed, "God, bless this food and this time with Carlos," he would have completely missed out on seeing God at work! That's why we must boldly ask for specific things—even little things!—and watch God reveal His mighty power. He delights in answering our prayers.

The Holy Spirit communicates with us through thoughts, feelings, signs, and even gentle nudges deep within us. So we must be still, listen, watch, and be ready to hear His voice.

God desires to guide us in every aspect of our lives. Whether it's deciding what to wear, which friend to hang out with, or how to handle a tough situation, let's involve God in it all. Pray boldly, ask Him specific questions, listen patiently, and trust that He will respond.

GOD, I'M SO GRATEFUL THAT YOU WANT TO ANSWER

MY BOLD, SPECIFIC PRAYERS. PLEASE OPEN
MY HEART AND MIND TO HEAR YOUR VOICE,
TRUST YOUR GUIDANCE, AND BELIEVE
IN YOUR LIMITLESS POWER. AMEN.

HOPE ON SAFARI

> The LORD hears his people when they call to him for
> help. He rescues them from all their troubles.
>
> PSALM 34:17

Let me tell you a story that will have you holding your breath and praying like never before. Picture this: My family and I were in Uganda, headed out on a sunset safari in an open-air vehicle. To say we were excited would be an understatement!

We saw animals ranging from graceful giraffes to playful elephants. But there was one thing my wife, Heather, really wanted to see. So she sent up a quick prayer to God: "Thank You for the chance to witness your magnificent creation, Lord. Would you please also show me a lion perched in a tree? That's a sight I would love to behold!"

You won't believe what happened next. Literally three minutes after Heather prayed, we stumbled upon not just one, but two lions gracefully resting on tree branches. Talk about incredible!

But then the adventure took an unexpected turn. Our vehicle broke down directly under the tree where one of the lions was perched. There were no other safari vans around, and we had no cell service. Gulp.

My daughters' eyes went wide with fear. In that moment, we turned

54

to the only source of strength we had left—prayer. Heather led the way, earnestly crying out to God for His intervention and protection.

And guess what? Again, her prayer was answered within minutes. A ranger arrived on an ATV, armed and ready to protect us. God had orchestrated the perfect rescue mission. Now all we needed was a way to get safely back to our hotel rooms.

As the night grew darker, the lion began to stir. It climbed down and started walking toward us. To our relief, the lion veered behind the vehicle and disappeared into the tall grass. Except now we had a new problem: we had no idea where the lion was. It could be anywhere in the pitch-black night.

The ranger told us to climb onto the roof of our vehicle. We did as we were told and huddled together there. Then we heard it—the sound of the lion approaching. The guide informed us that it was hunting, searching for its next meal. Time seemed to stand still as we waited.

Finally, after what felt like an eternity, a working vehicle showed up. One by one, we climbed down from the roof, ran to the waiting vehicle, and headed back to safety.

Fam, let us never underestimate the power of prayer. We have access to a God who brings us limitless hope, whether we are asking to see a lion or asking to not be eaten by one! May we always remember that God is our refuge and strength, our ever-present help at all times.

GOD, THANK YOU FOR BEING MY PROTECTOR AND DELIVERER.

WHEN I AM IN NEED OF RESCUE, HELP ME TRUST IN YOUR FAITHFULNESS AND TURN TO YOU IN PRAYER. AMEN.

COMPLETE FAITH

> The greatest person in the kingdom of heaven is
> the one who makes himself humble like this child.
> MATTHEW 18:4 ICB

A while ago, I was going through a tough time. My speaking tour got canceled, and money was tight without that paycheck. One day my son, Losiah, caught me with my head in my hands, eyes cast down. "Dad, what's wrong?" he asked.

I didn't want to burden him with money stuff, but I also wasn't going to lie to him and say everything was fine. Especially not after he'd caught me moping around like Eeyore. So instead I said, "Nothing for you to worry about, Losiah."

Yeah . . . he wasn't going to buy that answer either. He kept asking what was wrong. Finally, I opened up.

Now, guess what Losiah said? He asked me a simple question that caught me by surprise. He said, "Dad, have you asked God for the money?" At first, I thought it was a bit silly. But I soon realized Losiah was onto something. Why *hadn't* I prayed to God about it? So that night, I humbly asked God to provide the money we had lost.

The very next morning, a pastor friend called. "Carlos! Hey, man. I've got an event coming up that I *know* you'd be the perfect speaker for. Are you available?" What?! You bet I was available! And you want to know the best part? The payment for that event covered the entire cost of the canceled tour! I was so thankful. I rushed to Losiah's room, waking him up to share the incredible news.

I was expecting him to match my level of excitement and then some. But his reaction surprised me yet again. He smiled and said, "Of course He did," before rolling over and falling back asleep. No whoops. No cheers. Not even a high five. Losiah wasn't surprised *at all*.

Really, I shouldn't have been surprised either. God has always done amazing things, often meeting exact needs. Like when He gave a starving woman and her son the exact amount of flour and oil they needed to eat bread. And when Jesus turned one basket of food into lunch for over five thousand people. And if I had listened to Jesus, I would have also known to trust Losiah's complete faith. Jesus said there's a lot adults can learn from kids.

So, my awesome friends, no matter what challenges you face, ask God and trust He will answer. Keep your hope strong, and never forget that God's power is greater than anything in the whole wide world. And He is listening to you!

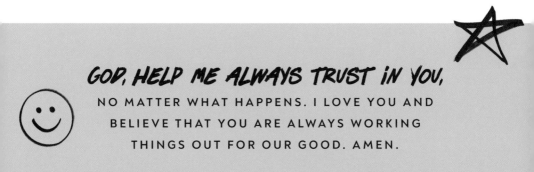

GOD, HELP ME ALWAYS TRUST IN YOU,

NO MATTER WHAT HAPPENS. I LOVE YOU AND BELIEVE THAT YOU ARE ALWAYS WORKING THINGS OUT FOR OUR GOOD. AMEN.

POWER OF PRAYER

Pray continually.

1 THESSALONIANS 5:17 NIV

When I learned that my friend Tonee was really sick, I wanted to do something. So I did what I hoped any friend would do for me if I were as sick as Tonee was. I tossed my clothes in a bag, jumped in my car, and drove eight hours across a few states to be by his side as I prayed for him.

It didn't make a lot of logical sense. I mean, I could pray for Tonee from anywhere in the world, right? And of course, in the back of my mind, I wondered if my prayers would make any difference. But then I thought, *What if they do? What if God does heal Tonee?*

If there was *any* teeny tiny percent of a chance that my prayers would help, why would I *not* pray with everything in me? Of course, if I prayed and God didn't heal Tonee, I would be sad. But I would at least get to be in God's presence with Tonee. And connecting to God in prayer always brings me comfort.

So I prayed. Then I prayed some more. My prayers might have sounded crazy to some people, especially doctors and nurses. But you know what? I didn't want to live in a "What if it doesn't happen?" mentality.

Throughout my life, many of my prayers haven't been answered the way I wanted. Like the prayers I've sent up for my dad's mind as he battles dementia. It can be tough, but I refuse to stop praying just because the thing I'm asking for may not happen. Why? Because it costs me nothing to pray, and besides, what if it does happen? What if God *does* bring healing?

You know, there's a verse in the Bible that has become so meaningful to me. It's found in 1 Thessalonians 5:17, and it simply says, "Pray continually." This verse reminds us that prayer is not a one-time solution or a last resort. It's an ongoing conversation with God. It's about staying connected to Him, seeking His will, and finding hope in His promises.

Sadly, my friend Tonee's health was not restored. As much as I had hoped in a different outcome, I am forever grateful for the time I had by Tonee's side. And I know that God really did heal Tonee, with the complete healing only possible in heaven. God doesn't always answer prayers how we expect. But He is always here with us working for our good in all things (Romans 8:28).

And even when we don't understand why things happen, just being in God's presence helps. Prayer can bring hope, comfort, and strength to our lives. It's a gift we can access anytime, anywhere, from the One who loves us unconditionally.

GOD, THANK YOU FOR THE INCREDIBLE GIFT OF PRAYER
THAT LETS ME CONNECT WITH YOU
ANYTIME, ANYWHERE. AMEN.

MILD FAITH TO WILD FAITH

The thief comes only to steal and kill and destroy; I have come that they may have life, and have it to the full.

JOHN 10:10 NIV

When I went camping with my family, I wanted to take a picture of the beautiful starry night. *Click!* Memory captured! But . . . I could only see a few stars in the picture. I was using this great new camera I had just bought. There *had* to be a way to capture what I was seeing.

I reached out to a photographer friend of mine, and his first question was this: "Is the camera in auto mode?" I looked at the settings, and sure enough, auto mode. My friend said, "Dude. There's no way to capture the fullness of the stars in auto mode."

He went on to talk me through *allll* the adjustments to make on my camera. Finally, after an hour of fiddling, my camera was able to capture *thousands* of stars, revealing the vastness of the night sky.

Fam, sometimes we live our lives like that camera, experiencing only a fraction of the hope God has for us. We're in "auto mode," content with just a few blessings and missing out on so much more. But here's the secret: we can switch from auto mode to manual mode in our connection with God.

Switching to manual mode means changing the way we look at

God and how we communicate with Him. It means sitting still and taking in the vastness of His plans for us. How do we make this switch?

1. *Turn down the volume.* Find moments of silence and solitude where you can focus on God and hear His voice.
2. *Pray for specifics.* Be specific in your prayers and trust that God is listening and working behind the scenes.
3. *Pray the promises.* When we align our prayers with God's promises, we tap into the power of His Word and see His blessings in our lives.

Friends, God has so much in store for each one of us. Don't settle for a life lived in auto mode. Switch to manual mode, change the way you connect with God, and open yourself to His limitless hope. The fullness of life is waiting for you!

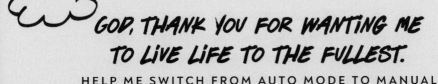

GOD, THANK YOU FOR WANTING ME TO LIVE LIFE TO THE FULLEST. HELP ME SWITCH FROM AUTO MODE TO MANUAL MODE IN MY FAITH SO I CAN CAPTURE THE ABUNDANT HOPE YOU HAVE FOR ME. AMEN.

THE POWER OF COMMUNITY

"I will give you back your health and heal
your wounds," says the Lord.

JEREMIAH 30:17

Have you ever experienced a moment when everything just seemed to fall into place? When hope burst through the darkest clouds, bringing light and joy? Well, let me tell you about a moment like that from my life. A moment that will leave you in awe of the power of prayer in community and the unstoppable force of hope.

I was at a conference, surrounded by music that stirs my soul. The band started playing a familiar tune, the one my band used to end our sets with. Suddenly, my phone buzzed. I couldn't believe my eyes. It was Larry, my guitar player from the old band. That would have been miraculous enough, but here's what's even more miraculous:

Larry had been battling COVID-19 for months. He had been on a ventilator and in a coma. We weren't sure if he was going to survive. I had been in contact with his family, offering love and support and prayers. I had also encouraged our community to pray for Larry, believing that the force of our prayers would be stronger together. But I hadn't heard from Larry since before he got sick, and *Larry himself was FaceTiming me*! During our song! A song with the lyrics, "The Enemy has been defeated. Death couldn't hold You down."

In between labored breaths, Larry whispered, "Thank you, Carlos. Thank you for praying for me and rallying your community to pray." I was overwhelmed, and all I could shout back at him was, "LARRY, THEY ARE PLAYING OUR SONG! YOU CALLED WHILE THEY ARE PLAYING OUR SONG!" In that moment, tears of gratitude flowed from both of us. Larry was out of the coma. The Enemy had been defeated. Death couldn't hold him down.

How incredible is that? God orchestrated this divine connection, reminding us of His love and the power of our prayers. I held up the phone, letting the music wash over Larry and his wife, Jessica. The melody became a declaration that Larry's life was a living miracle in progress.

Amigos, Larry's story proves that we are never alone in our struggles. We are a familia, bound by compassion, faith, and the incredible power of God's limitless hope. When we combine the power of our individual hope together through prayer, we can make miracles happen.

GOD, THANK YOU FOR THE GIFT OF COMMUNITY, FOR THE WAY YOU USE US TO BRING HOPE TO OTHERS. MAY THIS STORY INSPIRE ME TO BE AN AGENT OF HOPE IN MY OWN COMMUNITY, SPREADING YOUR LOVE WHEREVER I GO. AMEN.

IS WORRY CREEPING IN?

So don't worry about tomorrow. Each day has enough
trouble of its own. Tomorrow will have its own worries.

MATTHEW 6:34 ICB

I recently read this study that said 85 percent of the things we worry about never actually happen. And even for the remaining 15 percent, the majority of people said they handled it better than they thought they would. So basically, 97 percent of the things we worry about won't happen or won't be as bad as we imagine. That's a whole lot of unnecessary worry, my friends!

Worry is part of being human, but we don't have to let it control us and steal our hope. When worry creeps in, here are some ideas to overcome it:

1. *Name your worries.* List them on a piece of paper. Think about things you can do to reduce your worries, like studying for a test. Let God handle the rest of the list.
2. *Be still and pray.* In a quiet place, give God your worries as you take several deep breaths.
3. *Take care of your body.* Eating healthy foods and getting regular exercise releases chemicals in your brain that make you happy.

4. *Check your crowd.* Surround yourself with people who bring you hope and joy. Let go of the relationships that drain you.
5. *Ask for help.* If you feel worried a lot, tell an adult. You can also ask them to help you find a therapist. Therapy is not about being broken; it's about finding guidance and support.
6. *Shift your focus.* Take a moment at least once a day to praise God for His goodness and reflect on the things you're grateful for from the day.

When we choose to worry less and connect with God, we can experience His joy, hope, and peace. God wants us to enjoy our lives, to be present, and to find delight in Him. Besides, how often does worrying about something change the outcome? I'll give you a hint: never. Can you imagine worrying about what's going to happen to your favorite character in a book or TV show? What good would that do? You just need to keep following the story and see what happens! The same is true between us and God. Find comfort in knowing that He is in control, and let it go.

Remember, amigos, worry may try to knock at your door, but don't let it in. Turn to God. Ask Him to help you choose joy, embrace the present, and trust in His goodness. He's got this!

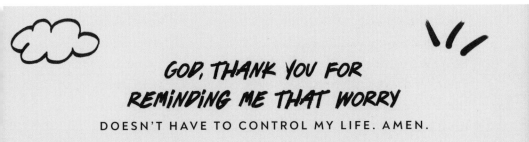

GOD, THANK YOU FOR
REMINDING ME THAT WORRY
DOESN'T HAVE TO CONTROL MY LIFE. AMEN.

BIG EMOTIONS

Give all your worries and cares to
God, for he cares about you.
I PETER 5:7

I go around and preach at different churches, and one night after my message to a room of full-grown men, I invited them to come forward for prayer. And boy, did they come! We prayed together, and it got *emotional*. Fathers asked for healing in their broken relationships. Sons confessed that they had been struggling with sins and addiction. Athletes and leaders who usually stood tall were showing their strength by kneeling down on the ground. These men were bravely opening their hearts and letting the tears flow out.

Bringing all your thoughts and feelings to God in prayer is muy importante. Yeah, I know, it can sometimes feel weird or scary to pour out everything to God. But guess what? He's not surprised or hurt by your emotions or doubts. He's right there, ready to listen and help you through it all.

Emotions can give us a glimpse into the wounds that need healing.

God gave us emotions; they are not separate from Him. When I see my family members who live far away, I feel big emotions. When I gaze out at a beautiful beach, I feel big emotions. When the Atlanta Falcons win a football game, I feel big emotions. And when I read the Bible and encounter God's truth, you better believe I feel big emotions too!

So don't detach the emotions that God has given you. He created each member of your family, He created water and sand and sea-gulls, and He created your incredible mind. He can even use things made by us, like sports, music, and art, to help us feel His presence. Your emotions can lead you toward God, guiding you in your journey with Him.

And guess what? God is not scared of your doubts either. He welcomes them with open arms. You can take your doubts to Him in prayer, laying them out honestly before Him. He longs to provide us with the reassurance, wisdom, and understanding we seek.

Allow your big emotions to draw you closer to God—not push you further away. Bring it all to God in prayer: your joys, your fears, your doubts, and your hopes. He wants to hear it all because He cares for you. Don't hold back, fam. Pour out your heart to Him and trust that He will guide you, heal you, and bring you hope.

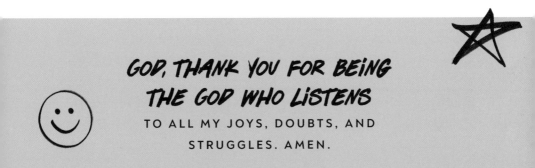

GOD, THANK YOU FOR BEING THE GOD WHO LISTENS TO ALL MY JOYS, DOUBTS, AND STRUGGLES. AMEN.

OUR WHIMSICAL GOD

A cheerful heart is good medicine.

PROVERBS 17:22

You probably know a lot about God. But here's something you might be surprised to learn: He's FUNNY! Yes, you heard it right. Our almighty, all-powerful God who created the heavens and the earth, who parted seas, who stops the sun from moving in the sky and raises people from the dead, also *loves* to bring laughter and joy into our lives. Let me share a cool God story with you that will make you giggle.

My wife and I were returning from Ireland, feeling exhausted and grumpy. I tried to cheer her up by cracking jokes, but she wasn't in the mood. I prayed, asking God for some relief to this exhaustion and stress. And then, there it was: a P.F. Chang's inside the airport. She *loves* their lettuce wraps. We walked in, and I thought, *Thank You, Jesus!*

Still, she was a bit grumpy, so I decided to tell her a funny story. It was about a time when I was leading worship, and my percussion player forgot his egg shaker. We had to rush to the music store, but all they had was a shaker in the shape of a banana.

We had no choice. We needed a shaker. So throughout the worship set, I keep looking over to see this guy banging on the drum with one hand and shaking that banana with the other. I thought it was hilarious. But guess what? My wife didn't find it funny at all. Bummer!

Then something unexpected happened. The waitress brought the check, and what do you think was on top? A fortune cookie, of course! I cracked it open, and there on the tiny slip of paper was one word: *banana*.

BANANA?! I freaked out and showed my wife. Suddenly, she burst into laughter and said, "We serve a whimsical, fun God."

See, my friends, if we only ask God to show up in serious moments, we miss half of who He is! That fortune cookie message became a daily reminder for me that God is always with us, even in the little things—and especially in the whimsical things. I framed it and placed it next to my bed. Every morning, when I wake up, I roll over and see it as a playful invitation from God to enjoy life and find joy in the unexpected.

All we have to do to experience God's delightful whimsy is connect with Him through prayer. When we bring Him in to every part of our lives—good, bad, and ridiculously hilarious—we more fully live into the knowledge that our God is a fun God who loves us deeply.

GOD, THANK YOU FOR BEING A WHIMSICAL AND FUN GOD

WHO BRINGS LAUGHTER INTO MY LIFE. TEACH ME TO CONNECT WITH YOU FULLY, NOT JUST IN THE SERIOUS MOMENTS, BUT IN THE EVERYDAY JOYFUL MOMENTS TOO. AMEN.

HOPE IN THE DARKNESS

Weeping may stay for the night, but
rejoicing comes in the morning.

PSALM 30:5 NIV

Have you ever seen a video of an astronaut walking on the moon? They move slowly in huge space suits that keep them separate from the universe outside. To me, that's what depression feels like.

Now, don't get me wrong. Being an astronaut would be super-cool, not depressing at all. Zero gravity sounds like a good time. But I've battled seasons of depression my whole life, and in those seasons, everything seems muffled and distant. People's voices sound far away, and even hugs don't reach my heart. Hope feels out of reach—like I'm trapped in a space suit.

If you can relate, there's something you need to remember: depression affects your brain, not your soul. During seasons of depression, your soul is intact and holds joy.

Ask God for help. The joy of the Lord can be your strength. It may not feel like it, but His joy is always in you, waiting to shine through. And the only way to find it is to let Him into your heart. Like the tether connecting an astronaut to their spaceship, prayer connects us to God, our source of joy and hope.

Here are some tips that I've found helpful when depression raises its ugly head:

1. *Be patient.* You won't feel better overnight, but change will come gradually. Journal your thoughts and feelings. Someday, you can go back and read what you wrote and see how far you've come.
2. *Create a laughter list.* Write down things that make you laugh and moments that bring a smile to your face. This is a reminder that joy is always within reach, even in the toughest times.
3. *Get fresh air and sunlight.* Spend time outside, soak up that sunlight, and let nature's beauty lift your spirits. Exercise, too, can work wonders for your mood and well-being.
4. *Reach out for help.* Getting help doesn't make you weak.` And struggling in silence isn't better for anyone. Be courageous and talk to a trusted adult who can help you find a therapist.

Depression is a season, and it *will* pass. Even if it's been weighing you down for a long time, it is *not* your forever. And throughout it all, God is right there with you. He's not sitting outside your space suit but inside it, right next to you.

Keep holding on to hope, even in the midst of darkness. The morning of rejoicing is on its way.

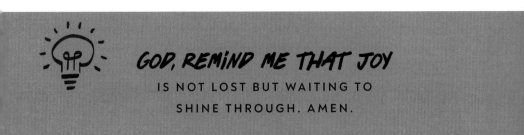

GOD, REMIND ME THAT JOY
IS NOT LOST BUT WAITING TO
SHINE THROUGH. AMEN.

UNTOUCHABLE HOPE

> And so, Lord, where do I put my
> hope? My only hope is in you.
> PSALM 39:7

Let me tell you something straight up: no one can steal your hope. Seriously! They can try, but guess what? They can't have it! And you know why? Because your hope comes from a limitless source, the one and only God.

Somebody might try to take your hope today, intentionally or unintentionally. Maybe someone is spreading rumors or saying hurtful things about you, trying to make you doubt yourself. Or maybe you face constant comparison on social media, feeling like you'll never measure up. But remember, your hope is grounded in something much stronger—God's love and promises for you. And you have the power to keep your hope safe and secure. Here's how:

1. *Boss 'em.* You're the boss of your own hope, my friend. Don't let anyone else control it. If someone tries to steal your hope, fire them as your hope keeper. They never should have had the job in the first place. You decide who holds the key to your hope, and it's definitely not them.
2. *Block 'em.* Use your hands, use your thumbs, but most importantly, use your voice. Repeat these words before, during, and after any interaction: "You can't have my hope!"

When you let those words sink in, it's like putting up a shield that keeps your hope safe and secure. Your hope is untouchable.

3. *Bless 'em.* Now, this one might seem a little strange, but trust me, it's powerful. When someone tries to steal your hope, do the unexpected—bless them. Pray for them to experience joy and abundance. Show kindness by buying them an ice cream at lunch. By blessing them, you take away their ability to steal your hope.

So remember these three steps, my awesome amigos and amigas: boss 'em, block 'em, and bless 'em! With these tools, you're equipped to protect your hope and keep it shining bright.

But here's the best part: Even when others try to take your hope, you have a secret weapon that's always available—prayer! When you feel your hope running low or being threatened, turn to God in prayer. He is the source of all hope, and He's got an unlimited supply just for you. Talk to Him, pour out your heart, and let Him fill you up with His everlasting hope.

Now go out there and rock this day with your unstoppable hope! Remember, they can't have your hope because it's in the hands of the almighty God. You're amazing, and I'm cheering you on. ¡Adiós!

GOD, THANK YOU FOR BEING THE SOURCE OF MY HOPE

THAT NO ONE CAN TAKE AWAY FROM ME. WHEN PEOPLE TRY TO STEAL MY HOPE, REMIND ME TO TURN TO YOU IN PRAYER. AMEN.

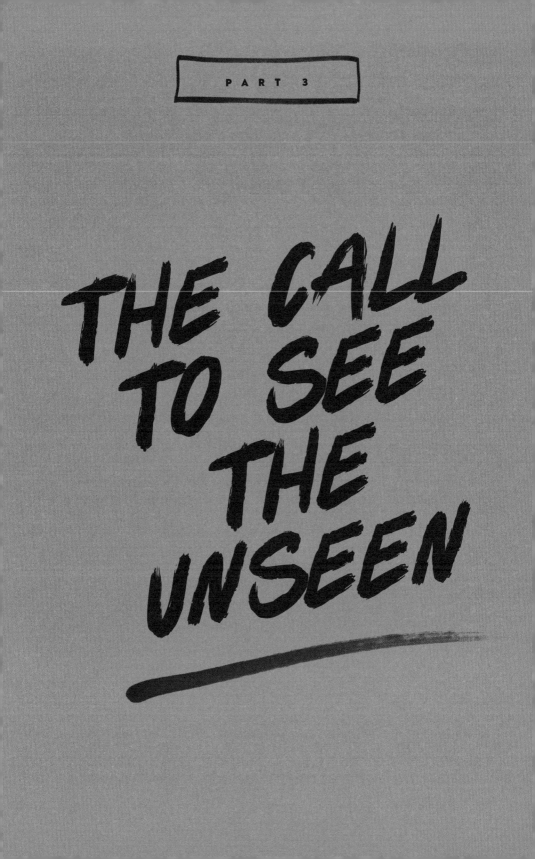

PART 3

THE CALL
TO SEE
THE
UNSEEN

PEOPLE MADE INVISIBLE

> The LORD doesn't see things the way you see
> them. People judge by outward appearance,
> but the LORD looks at the heart.
>
> *I SAMUEL 16:7*

When I was a kid, I *loved* watching sports with my family. I would get so into the games, jumping from my seat and shouting at the TV screen right alongside my dad. We could go from the top of the world one moment to pounding our fists on the couch cushions the next. It was a wild ride.

Recently, I came across a video that had me in my feelings, bringing me back to the joy of those days.

It was this incredible video of Joel Selwood, a professional Australian football player (that's *soccer* for all my American friends). During the victory celebration after an important match, Joel spotted Sammy, the team's water boy, in the crowd on the sidelines.

What struck me was that Joel *saw* Sammy as a valuable part of the team. Joel invited Sammy onto the field to share in the celebration. It was a beautiful act of inclusion, and it got me thinking about the power of seeing people who usually go unnoticed.

Many people feel invisible. People who have moved here from a different country, people with disabilities, people without a home, people who think or feel or believe differently than everyone around them. They live on the sidelines of society, often going unnoticed or unheard. But here's the thing: each one of us has the ability to see them, to truly see their worth, their struggles, and their dreams. When we open our eyes and acknowledge their existence, we ignite a flame of hope within them.

Advocating for marginalized people starts with seeing them as individuals, not just statistics or labels. It's about recognizing their humanity and standing alongside them in their journey. When we see the unseen, we become hope dealers, spreading love, acceptance, and justice in a world that desperately needs it.

The Bible says that God sees us all for who we are in our hearts. And He thinks we are all valuable. God sees both the star player and the person handing out water on the sidelines. And He thinks they are both equally awesome. As we follow Him, we can see others with that same love and value.

Remember, my friends, you have the power to bring hope to this world. Start by seeing the unseen, and together, let's create a more inclusive and loving society. Keep shining your light, and never underestimate the impact you can make.

GOD, THANK YOU FOR OPENING MY EYES TO SEE

THOSE WHO OFTEN GO UNSEEN.
HELP ME VALUE THE WORTH IN EVERY
PERSON I ENCOUNTER. AMEN.

A FIGHT FOR FAIRNESS

Speak up for those who cannot speak for themselves;
ensure justice for those being crushed. Yes, speak up
for the poor and helpless, and see that they get justice.
PROVERBS 31:8–9

I don't know about you, but my family is obsessed with Marvel movies. We love seeing Captain America and Spider-Man and Thor in action, using their powers to save the world. But you know what? There are real-life heroes too, and they don't need fancy suits or super strength. They are regular people like you and me, who fight for what's right and spread hope in the world.

Back in the 1960s, there were these amazing heroes called the Freedom Riders. This was during the civil rights movement, a time when our country was all messed up with racism. Black people were tired of the segregation of public transportation. So the Freedom Riders, a mix of folks from different backgrounds, got on buses all over the southern United States to challenge those unfair laws that separated people based on their skin color.

It was pretty risky, but they believed in sticking together and doing things peacefully. They wanted a fairer and more inclusive society for everyone.

James Zwerg and John Lewis were two courageous Freedom

Riders. James was White and John was Black, and they were like a dynamic duo fighting for justice and equality. These guys faced some tough times. Not only did they ride together, but they were beaten up and thrown in jail together. All because they wanted to change the world.

Do you think the Freedom Riders got tired of this and gave up? Nope! They kept pushing forward with their heads held high. Their actions spoke loud and clear to the government, who soon outlawed segregation in transportation. It was a major victory for justice and equality. The Freedom Riders showed us that when we stand up for what's right, incredible things can happen.

So what can you do to be a real-life superhero today? I've got a few suggestions:

1. *Be aware and show kindness.* Take the time to listen to the stories of people who are treated unfairly. Try to understand what they are going through and how it feels.
2. *Speak up.* If you see something that's not right, don't stay silent! Use your voice to speak out against unfairness, racism, or any kind of mean stuff.
3. *Get involved.* Find ways to help local groups that stand up for what's right. Start or join clubs at school that raise awareness about these important issues.

Fam, you've got the power to make a difference. Keep spreading hope and fighting for fairness. Together, we can grab our capes and make the world a better place for everyone.

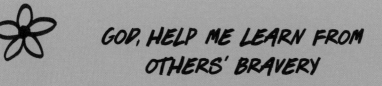

GOD, HELP ME LEARN FROM OTHERS' BRAVERY

AND USE MY VOICE AND ACTIONS TO BRING HOPE
AND JUSTICE TO THOSE WHO NEED IT MOST. AMEN.

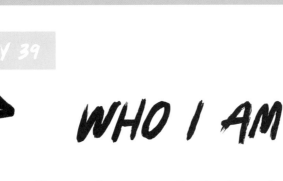

WHO I AM

There is no longer Jew or Gentile, slave or free, male and female. For you are all one in Christ Jesus.

GALATIANS 3:28

Growing up, I had my fair share of struggles and questions about my identity, especially when it came to being Black. But let me tell you, God has a beautiful way of teaching us to love ourselves the way He loves us—just as we are.

So far, I've told you about a lot of hope-dealing friends of mine. Today, I want to share a little bit about my own journey. I come from a mixed background. My mom is a light-skinned Mexicana, and my dad is a Black man from Panama. But when I was young, my dad told me that I was just Mexican. He said I wasn't Black because he didn't want me to listen to the racist messages about Black boys. He wanted me to feel like I belonged anywhere.

But it didn't work out like he intended. As I grew up in Atlanta, Georgia, I often felt torn between different worlds. Sometimes I even laughed at racist jokes without fully understanding their impact. But as I grew older, God opened my eyes to the importance of embracing all aspects of who I am.

When I was in the second grade, something happened that changed the way I thought about my identity. A classmate made a comment about my race. Around that time I also attended a mostly White church, where I formed some great friendships. But even there, some people seemed fixated on the color of my skin and the texture of my hair. All these experiences made me realize that my journey of self-discovery was just beginning.

Now, why am I sharing this with you? Well, it's because I want you to know that it's okay to ask questions about who you are. It's good to explore your identity and celebrate where you come from. In the Bible, we see how Jesus Himself embraced His Jewish identity unapologetically. He celebrated Jewish holidays, studied Jewish texts, and worshipped in synagogues. Jesus' identity mattered to Him, and it influenced everything He did. And that's a powerful lesson for all of us.

Like I said, it took me a long time to fully embrace my own Blackness. But having open conversations with my family and friends allowed me to explore and understand my identity better. We can do the same for others by providing an environment where they feel comfortable sharing their stories, traditions, and culture.

So my friends, embrace your heritage, celebrate your family's traditions, and be proud of who you are! And create safe spaces for honest conversations. When we take the time to understand and appreciate one another's experiences, we grow our empathy and unity.

GOD, THANK YOU FOR CREATING US

WITH DIVERSE BACKGROUNDS AND UNIQUE IDENTITIES. HELP US LOVE OTHERS AS THEY ARE AND ADVOCATE FOR THOSE WHO HAVE GONE UNSEEN. AMEN.

BOLD AND BRAVE ALLIES IN ACTION

Perhaps you were made . . . for just such a time as this?

ESTHER 4:14

In Amsterdam during World War II, a young Jewish girl and her family were in serious danger. The girl's name was Anne Frank. Ever heard of her? You probably have! She was someone who spread a lot of hope to others through her writings, despite having to hide out from the Nazis who wanted to take the Frank family to the cruel and deadly concentration camps.

How did they stay hidden? A woman named Miep Gies offered to let them live in a secret section of her home. Miep provided Anne and her family food, supplies, and hope. Despite the great dangers and risks involved, Miep showed up day after day.

Here's the thing you might not know—Miep didn't stop there. When the Nazis discovered the hiding place and arrested Anne and her family, Miep rescued Anne's now-famous diary and shared Anne's words with the world. By doing this, she helped shine a light on the experiences and struggles of those living in fear during the Holocaust.

Miep's actions remind us of the power of allyship. She listened, cared, and risked her own comfort to help others. She used her voice and took action, even when it was scary. She became an advocate for Anne and her family. We, too, can be good allies, standing up for those who are being threatened.

What does it mean to be an ally? Let's look to Miep's example for clues:

1. Miep listened to the cries of the Jewish people and took action. We, too, should be attentive to the struggles of others and ready to help.
2. Miep courageously spoke up, even in the face of big consequences. We can speak up for those who need a voice.
3. Miep took the time to understand the situation and gather information. We can follow her example by learning about different issues affecting marginalized communities.
4. Miep risked her own safety to help the Franks. While our risks might not be as dramatic as defying Nazis, it takes courage to stand up against discrimination. But remember, God is with us, just as He was with Miep.

Miep and Anne Frank's stories can inspire us to be bold and brave allies. So, my incredible friends, let's listen, speak up, educate ourselves, and take risks for the well-being of others. Together, we can make a difference and bring hope to those who need it most. Keep shining bright as allies in action!

GOD, THANK YOU FOR MIEP GIES
AND HER COURAGEOUS ACT OF ALLYSHIP.
HELP ME BE A BOLD AND BRAVE ALLY,
STANDING UP FOR THOSE IN NEED. AMEN.

HOPE THROUGH FRIENDSHIP

A friend is always loyal, and a brother
is born to help in time of need.
PROVERBS 17:17

I recently went with my family to Sea Island, Georgia, for a fun summer vacation. When we got to the beach resort, I immediately felt out of place. Was I the *only* non-White guest there? From what I could tell, the people who looked like me weren't guests. They were serving or cleaning.

Well, you can probably imagine that I wasn't able to relax on my family vacation after this realization. Instead, I went on a deep dive into the history of the racial divide in that area.

I learned about the plantations that used to be on the very land where I was now sipping my coffee. I learned about the rows of slave cabins still standing on the island. I visited the little-known historical site where, two hundred years earlier, a group of enslaved people from Africa had held hands and walked into the ocean together, drowning themselves to be free.

Instead of chilling at the beach with my family, I was educating folks on social media about the history of this section of the Georgia coast. And some people weren't digging it. They said I was wrong for talking about this time in history. That I was only causing more division. That I just wanted to make White people feel bad. Let me be real: their comments wore me out.

Then I got home, and—boom! Right there on social media, I saw two more videos of Black men being mistreated. I was d-o-n-e. Usually, I'm a pretty chill dude, but this time, I went on my Instagram Stories and let my passion and pain turn into angry yelling. I yelled about Black bodies being seen as less valuable than White bodies. I yelled about the fear I have to live with every day. I yelled about not being heard.

Now, most of my followers, listeners, and church audience are White. I'm honored to be a trusted Black voice in the larger community, and I take that role seriously. But it can be exhausting. And boy, was I tired, amigos. Tired of seeing people who look like me being mistreated. Tired of nothing changing. Tired of constantly explaining why the Black community is tired.

That's why when tough times like these happen, when our friends—Black, Brown, Indigenous, Asian—are exhausted, we need to reach out and ask one simple question: "How are you?" Then really listen. Listen to understand, not just to reply. Hearing the pain makes many of us uncomfortable, but that's okay. Sometimes, the greatest act of allyship is to just be there with them.

So let's build deep relationships with those who don't look, talk, worship, eat, or live like us. Let's be friends who really listen with love and understanding. Let's be allies who bring hope.

GOD, HELP ME BE THERE FOR MY FRIENDS

FROM UNDERREPRESENTED COMMUNITIES, ESPECIALLY WHEN THEY ARE HURTING. BRING HOPE AND HEALING THROUGH MY ACTIONS. AMEN.

WILD ADVENTURES AND BIG DREAMS

Our help is from the LORD, who made heaven and earth.

PSALM 124:8

What's the most adventurous thing you've ever done? Camping outside? White water rafting? Rock climbing? A few years ago, I found myself in the middle of "no-freaking-where" Alaska with the most unlikely group of adventure guides: a brilliant crew of Brown and Black kids from Brooklyn, New York. Kids who, until recently, had never even seen a mountain, much less spent ten days surviving in the wilderness.

How had we all gotten here? Well, each of our stories was a little different. But most of the kids' journeys were similar to what one young friend—let's call him Malik—described. Malik had always dreamed of climbing mountains and riding rapids, but he knew that adventures like that cost money. Money his family didn't have.

Then one day he heard about Brooklyn to Alaska, an organization that brings the magic of the great outdoors to kids like him—for free! Hope ignited in him for a world beyond the concrete jungle he'd grown up in. *No skyscrapers and smog?* he thought. *Sign me up!*

Soon, Malik found himself at the airport surrounded by a group of kids just like him, volunteers like me, and guides who had been in Malik's shoes as teenagers and now got to share the experience with others. As we all boarded the plane bound for Anchorage, Malik and the other kids exchanged nervous smiles. They weren't quite sure what to expect as the city faded away beneath the clouds.

Hours later, Malik and the rest of our group stepped off the plane and into the crisp Alaskan air . . . and then we were off. Hiking rugged trails, crossing gushing rivers, and setting up camp beneath the starry sky. Nature became accessible to Malik in ways he never thought were possible for him. As for me, I learned what "ice climbing" was. This was an adventure unlike any other!

As the days unfolded, Malik and the other kids discovered something extraordinary in the wilderness: themselves. They learned that they were strong enough to conquer challenging hikes and navigate through dense forests. They learned survival skills from experienced mentors. And they learned that they were not alone in this journey. They had a whole community of kids around them, supporting them through triumphs and setbacks.

Here's the best part: As they wrapped up the trip and traveled back to their favorite bustling cities, Malik and the rest of the kids brought back with them their newfound capabilities, grit, self-reliance, and deep connection to God's creation. They brought back hope that there is always more to discover, experience, and achieve.

And I came home filled with hope for all the kids like Malik out there, dreaming of adventuring.

GOD, THANK YOU FOR THE WONDERS OF YOUR CREATION

AND THE ONCE-IN-A-LIFETIME EXPERIENCES THAT SHAPE US. HELP ME FIND HOPE AND INSPIRATION IN ALL KINDS OF ADVENTURES. AMEN.

HOPE ON WHEELS

He lifts the poor from the dust and the needy from
the garbage dump. He sets them among princes,
placing them in seats of honor. For all the earth is
the Lord's, and he has set the world in order.

1 SAMUEL 2:8

My friend Don is insanely smart. He has a PhD in mechanical engineering from the Massachusetts Institute of Technology (MIT). He has patents galore (sixty, at my last count) in the biomedical field. All because he traveled the world, saw a problem, and decided to do something about it.

As he traveled to different places, Don saw people with disabilities—specifically, people who had a hard time walking—living without wheelchairs. He caught a glimpse of one woman, in particular, through the legs of passersby on a crowded street in Morocco. Instead of walking, she was dragging her body across the road with her fingernails. She couldn't walk but obviously didn't have the means to get a wheelchair.

That image changed Don's life.

Don went home, designed an affordable wheelchair, and shipped it to this woman in Morocco. Since then, Don has started an organization called Free Wheelchair Mission and provided wheelchairs to over 1.3 million people around the world. Their goal is simple: to give people independence by bringing mobility to the world.

Today's Bible verse says God raises the poor and lifts the needy. Free Wheelchair Mission embodies this truth, bringing hope to the most vulnerable and restoring their dignity. Because of the life-changing wheelchairs they manufacture, people who were stuck at home, lonely and suffering, can now get to school to get an education. They can get to a job. They can get to doctors' appointments and go see friends without any assistance.

Can you picture the smiles on the faces of the individuals and families who receive this gift? The tears of gratitude, and the sense of freedom they experience? These wheelchairs not only transform lives but also create ripples of hope in communities, inspiring others and sparking a chain reaction of compassion.

Don understands that this work isn't just about providing physical help; it's about addressing the emotional and spiritual needs of the recipients. Each wheelchair is a tangible representation of God's love and care, reminding people that they are seen and valued and that they can have abundant hope.

Remember, my friends, we all have the power to spread hope, advocate for the marginalized, and make a difference. It starts with seeing a need and using your unique talents to meet it. Let's keep the wheels of hope rolling and transform lives with God's love. ¡Vamos!

GOD, FILL MY HEART WITH COMPASSION

AND A DESIRE TO BRING HOPE TO THE MARGINALIZED. HELP ME SPREAD HOPE AND BE A VOICE FOR THOSE WHO NEED IT MOST. AMEN.

OUR AWESOME GIFTS

In his grace, God has given us different gifts for doing certain things well. So if God has given you the ability to prophesy, speak out with as much faith as God has given you.

ROMANS 12:6

Artist Danielle Coke felt like everyone was getting Dr. Martin Luther King, Jr. all wrong.

MLK Jr. was a radical disruptor. He challenged the standard ways people lived and rethought the way things were done. To many people, he was a criminal, not a hero. Danielle thought people were watering down Dr. King's fire.

So just before MLK Day in 2020, Danielle posted a drawing of a hand holding a protest sign that read "Just a reminder that MLK Jr. was not a quiet, gentle, law-abiding peacekeeper, but a radical disrupter who rejected passive inaction and fought for justice through civil disobedience." Danielle's powerful message lit a spark across the internet. Thousands of people started following her.

Then, in May 2020, a Black man named George Floyd was killed by police officers. Danielle again responded with messages of racial justice in her artwork.

One piece showed reaching arms of all skin tones with the word

"WORTHY" written across them. It powerfully communicated the beauty and equality of all people. Another work, titled "Anatomy of an Ally," showed different body parts like "a mouth to speak against injustice" and "ears to listen to the POC [people of color] experience." This gave people simple steps to take to begin their journey of allyship.

In a really dark and confusing time, Danielle's art gave people a place to start. It communicated simple, hopeful messages.

God has given us all talents. And He wants us to use them to bring hope. Think about the talents God has given you. If you can't think of any, ask some people who know you well to help you out. Because you *do* have some. The Bible says we all do!

Whether your talent is speaking or listening or singing, expressing yourself through art like Danielle, or something completely different, brainstorm ways you can use your talent to advocate for the people who need hope most.

GOD, THANK YOU FOR GIVING ME TALENTS.

HELP ME USE THEM TO BRAVELY STAND
UP FOR WHAT'S RIGHT. AMEN.

HEALING FOR CAMBODIA

> So you see, faith by itself isn't enough. Unless it produces good deeds, it is dead and useless.
>
> JAMES 2:17

My friends Don and Bridget Brewster are superheroes. They founded an organization called AIM—Agape International Missions. Their goal? To fight against modern-day slavery, a heartbreaking reality that affects millions of people around the world, including around ten million children.

One day years ago, Don and Bridget visited Cambodia for a mission trip. They traveled to fourteen different provinces and were met with kindness and warmth from the people there. Bridget and Don were given plenty to eat, even though the Cambodians themselves didn't have much. It was a powerful reminder that generosity and compassion know no boundaries.

But when they got home, they saw a chilling *Dateline* special about the very places they had just visited. The special exposed that children were being sold into slavery. It shook them to their core, and they knew they couldn't turn a blind eye.

Don and Bridget knew that faith without action is like a bicycle without wheels—it goes nowhere. So, they turned to prayer and fasting, seeking God's guidance. And you know what? God answered.

They felt a strong conviction to return to Cambodia and find places of aftercare and rehabilitation for those who had been rescued from slavery. They discovered a perfect property, a large house with beautiful surroundings. The only obstacle was the price. It was more than they could afford. But the landlady, moved by their mission, lowered the rent to make it possible.

They hired staff and trained them diligently for a whole year before opening their doors to rescued girls. At first, the girls who came carried wounds of anger and defensiveness. But through therapy, medication, and the unconditional love of family and God, they began to heal. The power of hope helped them return to their past environments and rescue other kids, spreading the light of hope to the hopeless.

Now, after sixteen years, the Brewsters have four restoration homes and nearly four hundred dedicated staff members. Their mission expanded beyond rescuing, and they now focus on prevention. They build schools, offering education as a key to a better future. They even built a kickboxing gym for young men.

Don and Bridget Brewster's story is a powerful reminder of the verse in James 2:17. Faith without action is useless, but when we combine our faith with action, miracles happen.

GOD, THANK YOU FOR THE INCREDIBLE EXAMPLE

OF DON AND BRIDGET BREWSTER. MAY THEIR STORY INSPIRE ME TO BE AN AGENT OF HOPE WHO MAKES A DIFFERENCE IN THE LIVES OF OTHERS. AMEN.

LILLIAN'S UNSTOPPABLE HOPE

For I am about to do something new. See, I have already begun! Do you not see it? I will make a pathway through the wilderness. I will create rivers in the dry wasteland.

ISAIAH 43:19

A while back, my family and I went on a life-changing trip to Uganda. We met a pastor whose church the Instafamilia had helped to build. We almost got eaten by lions. But the most life-changing part of the trip was meeting our host, Lillian, and hearing her story.

Lillian was our guardian angel in Uganda for four incredible days. She radiated joy and made sure we had food in our bellies, a roof over our heads, and love in our hearts. And here's the mind-blowing part: Lillian was once a child in need, and now she's changing lives herself. ¡Que increíble!

Every day when Lillian was a kid, she and her siblings went on a journey to fetch water from far away. The scorching sun beat down on them as they walked for miles, their tired feet trudging along the dusty path. But it wasn't just the lack of clean water that plagued their existence. The gnawing hunger in their bellies was a constant companion. Their meager meals consisted of discarded scraps they salvaged from their neighbors' garbage bins.

But everything changed when Lillian was eight years old. Her older half-brother, who was studying to be a pastor, introduced her to Compassion International, an organization that paired Lillian with a family across the globe who sent her money every month. With the support of her sponsor family, Lillian could attend school and eat meals chock-full of meat and vegetables. She even received encouraging letters from her sponsor.

When I think about Lillian, I'm reminded of a tiny seed that pushes through concrete to bloom into a beautiful flower. Her hope was like that seed, pushing through the tough soil of despair and hardship. She refused to let her circumstances define her. Instead, she walked to school every day, working hard to get an education so she could land a well-paying job to get her and her family out of poverty.

But wait, there's more! Lillian didn't stop at receiving hope—she became a hope dealer herself. She now *works* at Compassion International, where she gets paid to pour love into the lives of children just like her. And since she knows firsthand the power of a caring sponsor, she now sponsors a child who lives in Togo. She encourages him by addressing all her letters to him like this: "Dear His Excellency, the Future President of the Republic of Togo." Talk about speaking life into someone!

Lillian's story is a powerful example of God's promise in Isaiah 43:19. God is always working to do a new thing in our lives as we bring hope to others.

GOD, THANK YOU FOR LILLIAN'S INCREDIBLE STORY OF HOPE.

SHOW ME HOW I, TOO, CAN BE A HOPE DEALER IN MY LIFE AND IN THE LIVES OF OTHERS. AMEN.

HEARTS AGAINST HATE

Be strong and courageous. Do not be afraid or terrified because of them, for the LORD your God goes with you; he will never leave you nor forsake you.

DEUTERONOMY 31:6 NIV

Did you know that respect is a *big* deal in many Asian cultures? They believe in treating others with kindness and honoring their elders. Sadly, the same respect has often not been shown to them throughout history. For instance, during World War II, when Japan and the United States were at war, many Japanese Americans were shunned by their neighbors and forced to stay in internment camps. And most recently in 2020, the Asian community faced a whole new wave of disrespect. But this time, many people in the Asian American and Pacific Islander (AAPI) community have chosen to stand up and spread hope.

One of those people is high schooler Eugenie Chang. Shortly after COVID-19 spread throughout the world, she noticed something unsettling. People were pointing fingers at the Asian community, blaming them for the global pandemic. She watched in horror as even the most powerful world leaders stirred up hate! More and more news stations reported a surge in violence against Asian people, especially the wise elders who hold so much respect in their communities. And in her own California neighborhood, Eugenie started noticing snubs and insults and feeling afraid to walk down the street.

But here's where the story gets crazy hopeful: Eugenie decided to become a voice for the voiceless. She started a nonprofit organization called Hearts Against Hate, with a mission of getting kids and teens involved in the fight for racial equity. So far, over six hundred volunteers around the country have joined her cause! And together they've also handed out over 1,500 packages filled with safety gadgets to protect the elders in the AAPI community.

How can you lend your voice to the fight against hate? There are a few simple ways:

1. *Educate yourself.* Take the time to learn about the AAPI community's rich history and contributions to America.
2. *Speak up.* If you witness acts of hate or discrimination, use your voice to speak out and spread love instead.
3. *Extend kindness.* A simple smile, a friendly hello, or a helping hand can make a huge difference in someone's day.

The Bible tells us that God will give us strength and courage to do His righteous work. Sometimes that work is as simple as lending our voices to a cause like Eugenie's. Together, we can build a world where no one feels afraid and everyone feels valued and respected. Let's stand with the AAPI community, unleashing hope and celebrating their unique strength.

GOD, THANK YOU FOR THE AAPI COMMUNITY.

HELP ME USE MY VOICE TO SPREAD AWARENESS AND HOPE FOR A MORE RESPECTFUL WORLD. AMEN.

A VOICE FOR THE ENVIRONMENT

And what does the LORD require of you? To act justly
and to love mercy and to walk humbly with your God.

MICAH 6:8 NIV

You may not know this about me, but I basically live on a farm. But, like, a city farm. I'm sure it wouldn't pass as a real farm to some folks, but we have chickens. And beehives. And we grow things like radishes and kale and strawberries. So a farm.

I can't tell you how rewarding it is to get my hands dirty and see just what Mother Nature can do. But my love for the environment pales in comparison to that of a young warrior for justice and change, Ta'Kaiya Blaney.

Ta'Kaiya is a passionate advocate for the environment and for the rights of Indigenous people like her. Growing up as a member of the Tla'amin First Nation from the Salish Sea in British Columbia, Canada, she witnessed a lot of environmental destruction that made her say "enough." Industries used and abused her land's natural resources: wild salmon, cedar trees, rich soil. She felt a deep calling to protect and restore what had been taken away.

Filled with hope and determination, ten-year-old Ta'Kaiya began to use her talent as a singer and songwriter to raise awareness about these pressing issues. She's been doing this work ever since. Ta'Kaiya

believes that songs like her "Shallow Waters" and "Turn the World Around" have the power to inspire change. And wow, does she make a difference!

Through her heartfelt songs and speeches, Ta'Kaiya captures the attention of people around the world. She stands up against the construction of oil pipelines, believing that they pose a dangerous threat of oil spills that will pollute the beautiful waters that the Indigenous communities depend upon for resources. She also has become an advocate for the rights and safety of other Indigenous children.

Ta'Kaiya has spoken at international conferences, shared her stories with the media, and ignited a fire in the people who follow her on social media. She shows us that hope isn't passive—it's active. And that you don't have to wait until you're a certain age to take action. Hope requires us to step out of our comfort zones, raise our voices, and fight for what we believe is right. The Bible tells us that God requires the same: to *act* justly.

Ta'Kaiya embodies these words, demonstrating that through our actions, we can bring about meaningful change and be agents of hope in the world.

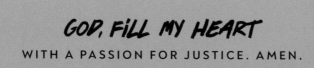

GOD, FILL MY HEART
WITH A PASSION FOR JUSTICE. AMEN.

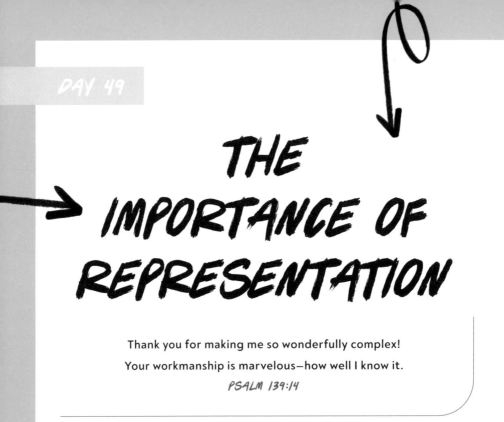

THE IMPORTANCE OF REPRESENTATION

Thank you for making me so wonderfully complex!
Your workmanship is marvelous—how well I know it.

PSALM 139:14

A little girl was settled on the couch, clutching her favorite stuffed animal tightly. The trailer for the new live-action remake of *The Little Mermaid* began to play on the TV in front of her. The vibrant underwater world unfolded before her with an array of colors. And then, Ariel came on-screen, face upturned, singing her famous "Part of Your World" line. The little girl's eyes grew wide, and she looked at her parent with shocked glee. Why? Because she saw a beautiful Black girl, with hair that resembled hers, portraying the iconic mermaid princess.

I've probably watched dozens of videos showing reactions like this. Videos of little Black girls all around the world feeling seen in a whole new way because of the 2023 remake of *The Little Mermaid*. I believe one of the most beautiful things in this world is helping people feel seen. It's like a spark that ignites joy and hope deep within their hearts.

Watching these videos, seeing these little girls' reactions of pure joy and surprise, moves something deep inside me. And it reminds me that we all have the ability to bring hope to others simply by acknowledging and celebrating their uniqueness.

You know, sometimes we prefer the original version of things. I get it. I prefer the original Coca-Cola. The original Jeep Wrangler. The original versions of all the songs in the Trolls movies. There's a nostalgia and familiarity that draws us in. But when we have the opportunity to remix something in a way that allows someone else to be seen, why not embrace it?

The truth is, when we make someone feel seen, we're shining a light on their worth and value. We're saying, "You matter. You are important." And that brings hope. Plus, we expand our understanding and appreciation for the diverse beauty around us. It doesn't take away from what was before; it simply adds to the detailed tapestry of life.

God has created each of us uniquely and with great intention. When we celebrate and embrace the uniqueness in others, we are reflecting God's love and affirming His handiwork.

So go out there and make a difference by simply making others feel seen. Play sports or games that include everyone, no matter their abilities. Be the first to welcome a new kid in school or your neighborhood and ask them to play with you. Ask your friends from different cultures to share their unique family traditions. Embrace the opportunity to celebrate others and let the hope of God's love shine through you. Stay blessed!

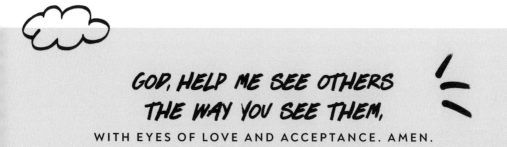

GOD, HELP ME SEE OTHERS THE WAY YOU SEE THEM, WITH EYES OF LOVE AND ACCEPTANCE. AMEN.

VOICES OF ADVOCACY

How wonderful and pleasant it is when
brothers live together in harmony!

PSALM 133:1

Back in my Lil 'Los years, I was in the school choir. I loved how my voice added to everyone else's made this big, powerful harmony that you could *feel* inside. But there's a different kind of harmony that's even more amazing: the power of voices coming together to create change. You can hear its melodious sound in one of my favorite true stories about the movement for women's right to vote.

Alice Paul and Lucy Burns were two best friends who joined forces and raised their voices together. As women in the early 1900s, they weren't given the same opportunities as men. They weren't allowed to buy a home, open a bank account, serve on a jury, or go to many of the best universities. They had hope for a society where women had the same rights as men. But for that to happen, there would need to be some women with political power. Which was a big goal considering women weren't even allowed to vote in elections!

So Lucy and Alice formed the National Women's Party, a political organization that fought for women's right to vote. They organized a march into Washington, DC, on the day before President Woodrow Wilson's inauguration. More than *half a million* people showed up!

Alice and Lucy were joining a courageous choir of voices made up of women like Elizabeth Cady Stanton and Susan B. Anthony, who had advocated before them. Their efforts paved the way for change, eventually leading to women gaining the right to vote. Talk about a triumph!

Amigos, you, too, have a voice, and it's powerful! One of the best ways to share your voice is to look for people who don't have a lot of power or rights in our society. Then, just like Alice and Lucy, you can join your voice with other voices. Amplify one another. Protest loud enough and long enough, until the people with the power to change the rules start to listen!

The Bible says it is wonderful when God's people live together in harmony. In order for that to happen, each person's unique role in that harmony must be seen and equally valued. So raise your voice. Call out injustices when you see them. Join forces and don't give up hope!

GOD, THANK YOU FOR SHOWING US
THE IMPORTANCE OF ADVOCATING FOR OTHERS.
HELP ME USE MY VOICE TO BRING HOPE AND
CHANGE TO THOSE WHO NEED IT. AMEN.

PART 4

THE WISDOM TO LEAD WITH LOVE AND GENEROSITY

TONY THE TURTLE

Share each other's burdens, and in this
way obey the law of Christ.
GALATIANS 6:2

Have you ever seen a group of turtles (a.k.a. a "bale" of turtles)? They are fascinating creatures. The other day, I saw an adorable video of turtles helping a fellow turtle in need. The lone turtle (let's call him Tony) was flipped over, shell down in the water. Then slowly, from the edges of the frame, eight to ten fellow turtles begin to swim toward Tony. They formed a tight circle around Tony and started to nudge, push, and jostle him until Tony flipped upright again!

Instead of leaving their friend behind, the other turtles gathered around, supporting him until loner Tony the Turtle was back on solid ground. Watching that video, I thought to myself, *What a beautiful example of love and generosity in action.*

Just like those turtles, we have the power to offer others hope by being loving and generous. When we see someone who is struggling, feeling down, or in need, we can step in and offer a helping hand. Listen, it's not always easy, but it is an important part of living out our faith and sharing with others the hope we have found in God.

Jesus tells us to look beyond ourselves and show love to those around us, just as Jesus has shown love to us. When Jesus was on earth, He went out of His way to help others. He stopped His sermon to heal a man who was paralyzed. He traveled to people's homes when they were sick. He stopped to help a blind man along His path.

So how can you follow Jesus' example? Start with paying attention to those around you. Look for the people who may be feeling like that turtle—turned around, struggling, scared, overwhelmed—and step in to help them get back on their feet. It could be as simple as offering a listening ear to a friend who is feeling sad or sharing your lunch with a classmate who forgot theirs. Small acts of kindness can have a big impact.

Just like the turtles who came together to help Tony, we can stand by others and offer support when they need it most. We can brighten someone's day, bring a smile to their face, and remind them that they are not alone. In doing so, we create a ripple effect of hope that can touch countless lives.

You have the power to spread hope through actions of love and generosity. Be the turtle that helps others back on their feet and watch as your acts of kindness create a brighter and more hopeful world.

GOD, THANK YOU FOR SHOWING US

WHAT IT MEANS TO LOVE AND BE GENEROUS. HELP ME OPEN MY EYES TO THE NEEDS OF OTHERS, AND GIVE ME THE COURAGE TO REACH OUT AND MAKE A DIFFERENCE. AMEN.

HOPE FOR HEROIC CAREGIVERS

Come to me, all of you who are weary and carry
heavy burdens, and I will give you rest.

MATTHEW 11:28

Let me tell you about mi mamá. She's a superhero, taking care of my dad, who has dementia. It's tough, really tough. But you know what carries her through? Connecting with God and reading His Word. The verse that brings her the most encouragement is Joshua 1:9. Be strong. Be courageous. Do not be discouraged. God is with you.

And you know what else makes a huge difference for her? It's when she hears from one of her sons, whether it's me or my brother Eddie. Something as simple as picking up the phone and calling her gives her something to look forward to, something to hope in.

Caregivers do *so* much. These are the people who love you, nurture you, and make sure you have everything you need. Whether it's parents, a grandparent, a foster parent, an aunt, or an uncle, every day they work hard. When you're sick, they comfort you. When you're scared, they calm your fears. They are always there, making safe and loving environments for you to grow and thrive in. They are everyday heroes.

But we have the power to bring hope and joy into the lives of our caregivers too. Remember what my mom said gave her the most hope next to reading Scripture? Hearing from her sons! That's right.

Just like your caregivers care for you, you can care for them too.

How, you ask? Well, there are so many ways! But here are just a few:

1. Say "thank you" for all they do.
2. Lend a helping hand around the house. Maybe it's tidying up your room, offering to help with meal planning or grocery shopping, or even taking on small tasks. Every little act of kindness makes a big difference.
3. Be understanding and supportive. Listen when they need to talk, offer encouragement during challenging times, and be there to share both the joys and the struggles.
4. Pray. Lift your caregivers up to God, asking for His guidance, wisdom, and strength as they navigate the challenges they face.

Let's honor these everyday heroes—our caregivers—by showing our appreciation, helping out, and being a source of support and encouragement. Together, we can bring hope and joy into their lives, just as they do for us.

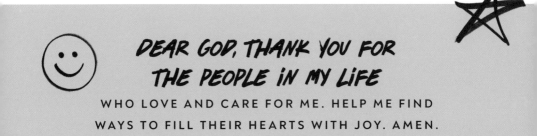

DEAR GOD, THANK YOU FOR THE PEOPLE IN MY LIFE

WHO LOVE AND CARE FOR ME. HELP ME FIND WAYS TO FILL THEIR HEARTS WITH JOY. AMEN.

AN EXTRA HOUR

This same God who takes care of me will supply
all your needs from his glorious riches, which
have been given to us in Christ Jesus.

PHILIPPIANS 4:19

In my life, the biggest lessons come during the seasons when it feels like all hope has run out. It was during one of those seasons—the most difficult time my family has been through—when a friend reached out to their followers on social media and asked them to step in and help us.

That act of love changed my life. When I thought there was absolutely no hope left, God used this friend—and all their many friends—to say, "Carlos, there's always hope with Me."

So when I came across Shanell's story, I knew it was time to pass that infinite hope along. Shanell had a young child and a husband in the military when she experienced her first seizure in March 2021. By June, she'd had over 250 seizures. She couldn't leave her home. She couldn't be alone. Someone had to be with Shanell at all times to keep her safe during her seizures. Shanell was asking for one thing: a dog trained to alert her family when she was having a seizure.

But a dog like that costs *a lot* of money. Tens of thousands of dollars. Shanell's support system had been able to raise over half of what she needed . . . but it wasn't enough. Shanell was losing hope.

And so, terrified of embarrassing myself, of failing, of looking like just another preacher guy asking for money, I took to Instagram and asked my followers if we could raise the rest of the money for Shanell to get her seizure alert dog. *Three* minutes after my request, we had raised another $1,000. I started thinking, *Wait . . . God can not only make this happen. He can make it happen* fast. So I made another request. I asked if we could raise the whole amount in two hours.

One hour later, Shanell had enough money to get her dog.

So now I had to find out what God could do with that extra hour. I knew Shanell needed more than just a dog. She would need help with medicine, doctor visits, special assistance, and other things. So I asked my followers to keep dealing out hope.

By the next morning, people had donated a total of $50,000 for Shanell and her family. I realized this group I had gathered was more than a bunch of random people giving me the occasional Like. We were an Instagram family—an Instafamilia.

Now, hoping in God doesn't necessarily mean you get $50,000. But God *will* blow past the boundaries of your hopes. That day, God came through. Shanell got the help she needed. And I found a hope on *fire* to keep this "Instafamilia" thing going. Since that day, I've done a bunch more Instafamilia fundraisers. Each and every time, God shows up *BIG*.

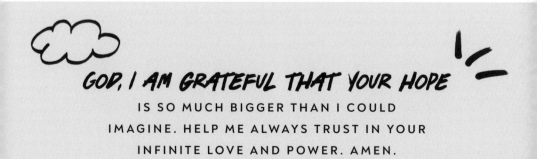

GOD, I AM GRATEFUL THAT YOUR HOPE
IS SO MUCH BIGGER THAN I COULD
IMAGINE. HELP ME ALWAYS TRUST IN YOUR
INFINITE LOVE AND POWER. AMEN.

THE JOY OF GIVING

Each of you should give what you have decided in your heart to give, not reluctantly or under compulsion, for God loves a cheerful giver.

2 CORINTHIANS 9:7 NIV

My friend Jessica is all about giving and helping others. She believes that when we give, something amazing happens inside of us. And trust me, she knows what she's talking about.

You see, Jessica Jackley started this organization called Kiva. She wanted to find a way for regular people like you and me to help entrepreneurs all around the world. A woman in Fiji who needs just $900 to open a food stand business. A woman in the Philippines who needs $275 to raise and sell pigs. A man in Uganda who needs $4,000 to buy tuk-tuks—small open-air vehicles—to bring clean water to his community. These people have big dreams and excellente ideas, but sometimes they just need a little bit of money to get started. That's where Kiva comes in.

With Kiva, you can lend money to these entrepreneurs. And guess what? They pay you back over time as their food stand, pig farm, or tuk-tuk business takes off. It's like a loan, but a loan with a lot of heart. And here's the awesome part—Jessica and her team at Kiva have helped facilitate over $1.5 billion in loans! That's billion with a *b*!

But Jessica didn't stop there. She thought, *Hey, why should adults have all the fun? Let's get kids involved in making a difference too!* So she started another organization called Alltruists. They create subscription boxes filled with fun and meaningful volunteer projects for kids. With their boxes you can do things like plant a tree, write a welcome-home note to a newly housed family, make a pollinator hotel to help support local bees, or make a welcome gift for a refugee child who was recently resettled. Their mission is to "raise kind humans." How cool is that?

Giving is not just about the amount of money you have or the things you can do. It's about the attitude of your heart. It's about showing kindness, compassion, and love to others. Plus it feels good to help someone, to put a smile on their face, and to make their day a little brighter.

You might be wondering, *But Carlos, why does giving feel so good?* Well, fam, it's because we were created to love and care for one another. When we give, we tap into this purpose. We become part of something bigger than ourselves, a community that cheers for the same thing: lifting others up.

So let's be like Jessica and the incredible people at Kiva and Alltruists. Let's find creative ways to make a difference, whether it's through lending a helping hand, sharing our resources, or simply being there for someone who needs a friend. Together, we can change the world and feel great while doing it!

GOD, THANK YOU FOR THE GIFT OF GIVING.

SHOW ME HOW I CAN MAKE A DIFFERENCE, BIG OR SMALL, AND BRING JOY TO OTHERS—AND TO ME! AMEN.

THE POWER OF SEEING AND MEETING NEEDS

Love your neighbor as yourself.

LUKE 10:27

One day Heather and I were at the airport. We were in the security line, surrounded by people stressing about the time they had left to get on planes. Suddenly, Heather said, "Babe . . . empty your suitcase."

"Why?" I asked. I was confused and—I'm ashamed to admit—a little frustrated. "What are you talking about?"

Heather pointed at a woman a few spots in front of us who had all her belongings stuffed into a flimsy plastic bag. Heather had felt a tug in her heart, and she turned to me and explained that she wanted to give *my* suitcase to that woman who didn't have proper luggage.

I had no choice. I dropped my bags in the middle of the crowd of people and started emptying everything out.

As I hastily transferred my stuff—half into Heather's bag, half into my carry-on backpack—I could feel the gazes of curious onlookers. Within thirty seconds, my favorite suitcase had a new owner, and all my underwear had found a place in my backpack. But more importantly, Heather had once again seen someone who nobody else noticed.

Heather has a crazy Spidey sense for other people's needs. Sometimes being with her reminds me of the story Jesus told about the Good Samaritan. In the story, a Jewish man was beaten and left wounded on the side of the road. Many people passed by, but only a Samaritan stopped to help. Samaritans and Jews did not get along. Because they had different ideas about how to practice religion, the Jews looked down on the Samaritans. But this Samaritan saw the Jewish man's need and reacted with compassion, going above and beyond to care for him.

Just like the Samaritan, we can make a difference by seeing the needs of others and responding with kindness. There are people who may feel invisible or burdened by life's challenges. We have an opportunity to offer them some hope, extend a hand, and free them of their worries, even if it's only for a moment. It doesn't always require grand gestures; even small acts of compassion can spread hope and bring comfort. It might be offering a hug to someone who feels alone, donating gently used toys or clothes to kids in need, or writing a letter to a friend.

We truly can make a difference one small act of kindness at a time.

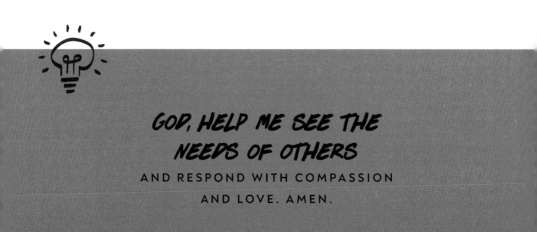

GOD, HELP ME SEE THE NEEDS OF OTHERS

AND RESPOND WITH COMPASSION
AND LOVE. AMEN.

HOPE BUILDERS

For we are co-workers in God's service;
you are God's field, God's building.
1 CORINTHIANS 3:9 NIV

A friend told me about a man called Pastor Bosco in Omokokitunge, a small village in Northern Uganda whose church had met under a mango tree for six years. Finally, they built a thatch (mud) structure and met inside that for four years. But fire and erosion kept damaging it. It was falling apart.

Pastor Bosco was a staple in this small village. He was not only running Sunday services but also training women in his community to run their own businesses. What's more, he gave them small loans and two pigs that they could raise and then sell for money to get those businesses started. So many men and boys had died in the war in Uganda that there were all these single women—mothers and grandmothers—left alone. Pastor Bosco and his church were giving them a way to provide for themselves. How cool is that?

Pastor Bosco sounded too good to be true, but I trusted my friend who told me about him. I started to ask around to see what it would take to give this incredible pastor a little hope with a new church building. An organization called ICM said they could do it for $15,000. I was like, "Wait, you can build an entire building for $15,000?"

To give you a little perspective, a typical church building in the United States costs many millions of dollars to build. But ICM said they could do it for a fraction of that cost. Even better, they could do it with all local workers, pouring money into the local Ugandan economy!

So I asked my Instafamilia to help out. And let me tell you, in just *ninety* minutes, we raised enough money for ICM to build that new church for Pastor Bosco! Then, over the next twenty-four hours, we raised enough for not one, not two, but *SEVEN* church buildings in seven different villages!

We gave seven congregations a sanctuary, a safe place to worship and dream. We didn't just build buildings; we built a foundation of hope, love, and community. These churches became more than a place for Sunday services. They became health clinics, schools, and community gathering spaces. They became centers for healing, education, and empowerment.

Six months later, when I finally met Pastor Bosco, his eyes sparkled with gratitude. It was like seeing hope come alive.

Amigos, when we come together, we can change lives. Whether it's donating your allowance or birthday money to your church, volunteering in the infant or preschool rooms, or using your talents in other ways like leading worship, you have the power to get involved and make a difference!

GOD, THANK YOU FOR SHOWING ME THE POWER OF UNITY.
HELP ME USE MY GIFTS TO BRING HOPE TO THOSE WHO NEED IT MOST AND MAKE A DIFFERENCE IN MY COMMUNITY. AMEN.

FIERCE LOVE

Love each other with genuine affection, and
take delight in honoring each other.
ROMANS 12:10

I have a lot of followers on social media. I'm not saying that to brag. I'm saying that to help you understand just how many different beliefs and perspectives I have in my "close circle." I have beliefs of my own. And I am very open about those beliefs. There are some things that most everyone who follows me agrees about: Jesus is awesome. Nature is awesome. Dogs are awesome.

But I have other perspectives that people sometimes take issue with. Some things are easy—and even fun—to debate. Like my belief that the Atlanta Falcons are the best sports team in the country. Some things are really hard to debate. Like the way Black people are treated differently just because of their skin tone. A lot of people who follow me don't agree that it's a real problem. And they are not afraid to let me know.

But honestly, I have it easy. My followers are pretty kind people. Their comments are nothing like the ones I see on other pages that just make my stomach turn. People making fun of someone's looks, intelligence, or loved ones because they disagree with a poster's opinion.

It's easy to get discouraged by all the hateful and rude commentary. It makes me sad because, as Jesus' followers, we have the incredible power to bring hope to everyone.

You see, my friends, it's not just our responsibility to bring hope to and pour out God's love on those we consider our friends. We're called to go *beyond* that—to extend hope and love even to those who may think differently or act in ways we don't understand. It's not our job to convict or condemn them; that's the role of the Holy Spirit.

That's why, when I witness fellow Christians using insults to wound others, it makes me cringe. The Bible tells us to love each other and take *delight* in honoring each other.

But hold on. This doesn't mean we abandon our convictions. It simply means we avoid the trap of slinging cheap insults at others. Instead, I've found that leading with love, especially toward those I disagree with, has been far more effective in bringing about meaningful conversations. Showing someone how much we love them, despite our differences, creates a safe space for connection.

You know, nobody can pull this off perfectly. That's why we need the Holy Spirit guiding us every step of the way. So let's wake up each day with a burning desire to love *all* people fiercely. Doing so will draw their hearts closer to ours much faster than any clever comeback or quick-witted comment ever could.

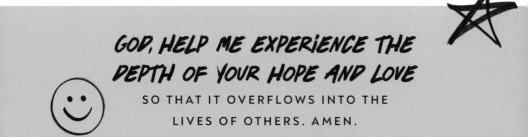

GOD, HELP ME EXPERIENCE THE DEPTH OF YOUR HOPE AND LOVE

SO THAT IT OVERFLOWS INTO THE
LIVES OF OTHERS. AMEN.

FROM DESPAIR TO HOPE

> Yet I still dare to hope when I remember this:
> *The faithful love of the LORD never ends! His mercies never*
> *cease. Great is his faithfulness; his mercies begin afresh*
> *each morning.*
>
> *LAMENTATIONS 3:21–23*

I was in Utah when I met and talked with an incredible hope dealer named Yves Dushime. Yves's mom was eight months pregnant with him when something unimaginable happened in their African homeland. The Rwandan genocide erupted, and in just a short time, over a million Rwandans lost their lives. Yves's parents fled their home and took refuge in a camp with other people forced from their homes.

Growing up in those refugee camps, Yves noticed something strange. Other families seemed to have more people. He wondered, *Where are our extra people? Where is my grandma? Where are my aunties?* His parents told him everyone in his extended family has been killed. Learning this filled Yves with hatred toward humanity. It felt like there was no hope to be found.

But Yves's dad, a pastor, saw their situation differently. He believed they were missionaries sent by God to bring hope to others in the refugee camps. Yves thought his dad was crazy at first, but then something amazing happened.

When Yves was around eleven, he received a gift. Through an organization called Operation Christmas Child, he received a shoebox filled with school supplies, toys, and gifts.

Inside that shoebox was a scarf that Yves still treasures to this day. And there was a little sticky note that said, "God loves you. Jesus loves you. I love you." He already knew the first two, but that last line lit a spark of hope within him.

Three years later, Yves found himself living in Buffalo, New York, when his family immigrated to the northern United States, and he really needed that scarf! Of course, Yves didn't mind the cold. His new home was fully furnished, with clean water flowing from *five* faucets. He never could have dreamed of this when he was in the refugee camps, without any running water!

Yves's story is a powerful testimony. He went from bitterness and despair to being filled with hope thanks to the power of God's unfailing love. And guess what? Just like the person who sent Yves that hope-filled gift, we have the power to share God's love. You never know whose life you might change.

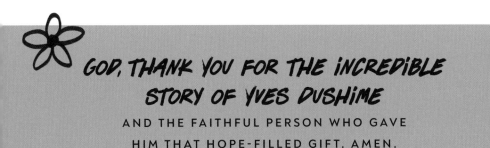

GOD, THANK YOU FOR *THE INCREDIBLE STORY OF YVES DUSHIME* AND THE FAITHFUL PERSON WHO GAVE HIM THAT HOPE-FILLED GIFT. AMEN.

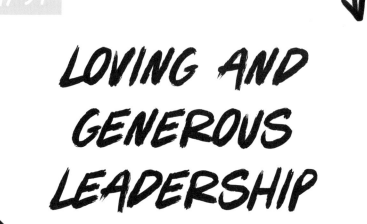

LOVING AND GENEROUS LEADERSHIP

Serve one another humbly in love.

GALATIANS 5:13 NIV

B ringing the good news and hope of God to everyone we meet is a great way to journey through life. But there's something important we need to watch out for. Sometimes we get this idea that we need to be the heroes, swooping in to save the day for others. And that is just *not* the way to go.

We can bring hope to others by leading with love and generosity—not thinking we're better than them.

When we step into a situation to bring someone a little hope, we have to be humble and ready to learn. Here's the truth, my friends: every person has something valuable to offer, something unique that we can learn from. We shouldn't think we know it all or that we're the saviors.

Recently, I went to Uganda, a country in Africa with an incredibly rich history and culture. But Ugandans struggle hard with poverty. Does that mean Uganda needs us to swoop in as "saviors"? No way! There are some incredibly brilliant, hopeful, innovative Ugandans who are already solving problems in their own country. Take Ugandan Brian Gitta for example.

Brian noticed a problem in his country—malaria. It was affecting so many people, especially children, and causing a lot of suffering. Brian decided to take action. He created a device called Matibabu, which uses a special light to diagnose malaria quickly and without the need for blood samples.

Could someone outside of the Ugandan community have come up with such a brilliant solution? Maybe . . . but probably not. Every group of people has experts, members of that group who really *know* the problems they face. Which is why it's so important that when outsiders come in, they don't try to show up and be the hero. Instead, they can walk alongside the locals and ask, "What do you need? How can I help?" That's when the love and hope of God spreads like crazy.

The Bible tells us to serve one another humbly in love. That's such a powerful reminder for us, especially when we're helping others. Serving one another humbly means letting someone else take the lead.

True service is not about boosting our own egos or feeling superior. It's about humbly serving others with love. It's about coming alongside them, listening to their stories, and valuing their experiences. When we serve others with humility and love, we create a space where genuine connection and transformation can happen.

So, let's look for ways to help others without assuming we're better than them. Let's build bridges of understanding and friendship in our communities. And let's seek out new ways to walk alongside others on this journey of life.

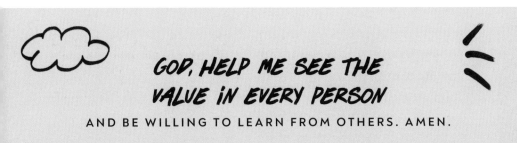

GOD, HELP ME SEE THE VALUE IN EVERY PERSON

AND BE WILLING TO LEARN FROM OTHERS. AMEN.

HOPE AMID CHAOS

Be strong, and let your heart take courage,
all you who wait for the LORD!
PSALM 31:24 ESV

Have you ever had a week where things seemed to go *all* wrong? Like, one bad thing happened, and then another, until you thought that *had* to be the end of it. But nope, there was more where that came from.

I sure have. It felt like everything was falling apart all at once. I mean, seriously, it was like a never-ending roller coaster of disasters. Car accidents, broken relationships, floods, sick pets, and even losing a favorite chicken and our beloved dog, Pope. And just when we thought things couldn't get worse, my wife, Heather, broke her wrist at the airport. Talk about a wild ride!

When that crazy week came to an end, guess what happened? Our community came together and covered the costs of the ambulance ride, hospital bills, car repairs, and even the flood damage. It was incredible! Our hearts were still hurting, but our friends shone hope into the darkness.

The Enemy wants to steal our hope and make us feel like we're trapped in a pit of hopelessness. But we don't have to stay there!

And when you have built strong relationships, you won't have to climb out of that pit alone.

But how do we get that community? It starts by being a good friend. Show up for your buddies when they are going through tough times. Be there to listen when they are having a tough day or help out when they are feeling overwhelmed with their chores. Do it without expecting anything in return, just because you genuinely care. Not every relationship will give you the same kind of support—but that's okay. Be patient and keep sowing seeds of kindness and love. If you want to have good friends, you first have to *be* a good friend.

So my friends, surround yourself with people who lift you up, support you, and remind you of God's love. They can be friends from church, from school, or from your team or club. Your community might include your cousins, aunts, uncles, or a favorite coach, teacher, or friend's parent. Then, when you're feeling hopeless, reach out to that community. Let them help you find the hope that seems lost.

Remember, you're not alone in this journey. God is with you, and so are your friends. Together, we can overcome anything that comes our way. Keep shining, amigos!

GOD, HELP ME BUILD STRONG CONNECTIONS WITH YOU

AND WITH OTHERS. GIVE ME THE COURAGE TO BE A GOOD FRIEND AND TO REACH OUT WHEN I NEED HELP. AMEN.

LIVES REVEALED

So encourage each other and build each other up, just as you are already doing.

1 THESSALONIANS 5:11

I recently came across a powerful video that touched my heart. It showed two sheriff deputies comforting a man who was going through a tough time. The man bravely expressed his need for a hug, and one of the deputies embraced him. That simple act of kindness brought tears to my eyes. It reminded me of how crucial it is to see the struggles people face and offer them hope.

In our lives, we encounter all kinds of people, and guess what? Every single one of them is battling something. Yes, it's true! Whether it's the people we love, the people we might not get along with, or even the ones who seem perfectly happy, there's always a battle going on beneath the surface. Maybe someone's parents are going through a separation. Maybe they are failing in school or struggling with their piano lessons. Maybe they have been bullied. These hard things can make us question our value and worth. Which is why every person needs to hear from you that they matter.

When you make someone feel seen and valued, you bring hope to their battle and remind them that they are valuable to someone. Because sometimes, those thoughts of being worthless or unloved get so loud that they are impossible to ignore. Sometimes people spend so long believing those lies that they don't want to live anymore. If you have ever felt that way, or know someone who has, it's so important to ask for help.

What help can you offer? There are a thousand small acts of kindness that have the power to change lives. You could reach out to encourage a store clerk, give a hug to your grandma, help your younger cousin with their homework, or even express gratitude to the person who is always delivering your family's packages and mail.

Remember, my friends, we should never judge someone's needs based on how happy or sad they seem. We must never assume that someone is okay just because they wear a smile, or that they want to be left alone because they seem sad. The truth is, we all wonder whether or not we matter. We all need encouragement and love, no matter what we're going through.

The Bible tells us to encourage each other and build one another up. So today and every day, let's make a commitment to show those around us that they matter, that they are cherished, and that we need them here.

And remember, YOU matter; we need YOU here too. Because you have the power to make a difference.

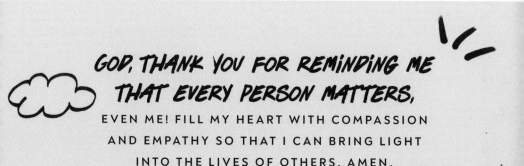

GOD, THANK YOU FOR REMINDING ME THAT EVERY PERSON MATTERS, EVEN ME! FILL MY HEART WITH COMPASSION AND EMPATHY SO THAT I CAN BRING LIGHT INTO THE LIVES OF OTHERS. AMEN.

SLOW CHECKOUT LANES

> Let us consider how we can stir up one another to love. Let us help one another to do good works. And let us not give up meeting together. Some are in the habit of doing this. Instead, let us encourage one another with words of hope. Let us do this even more as you see Christ's return approaching.
>
> *HEBREWS 10:24–25 NIrV*

I recently came across a story about a Dutch supermarket that introduced what they call "slow checkout lanes." Instead of rushing through the checkout process, the cashiers take their time scanning items and striking up conversations with the people checking out. And you know what? It's made a world of difference for the lonely and often unseen members of the community. It's given them a place to be heard and valued. Isn't that amazing?

You see, my friends, loneliness is a real struggle. Nowadays, with all the screens and social media, it's easy to feel disconnected from others. It's hard to feel the warmth of your grandma's hug through a screen. You don't get that comforting back rub from your best friend when you're feeling down. Deep down, we all long for genuine connections. We all want to be seen, heard, and loved for who we are. And that's where slowing down comes in.

When we slow down, we give ourselves the chance to really see the people around us. We notice a grown-up in our life could use a hug after a stressful day, our brother could use help with his homework, or the neighbor could use a friendly smile. It's in those moments that we have the power to make a difference.

So how can we slow down and connect? Well, let me give you a few ideas, mis amigos:

1. *Look up.* Put down your devices and notice the people around you, whether you're at school, in your neighborhood, or even in your own home.
2. *Listen.* When you're talking to someone, give them your full attention. Listen with your heart, not just your ears.
3. *Volunteer.* Whether it's serving at a local shelter, helping a neighbor with their groceries, or participating in a community project, these acts of kindness not only bring hope to others but also fill our own hearts with joy.

When we slow down, we create space for genuine connections. And in those connections, hope abounds. We experience the joy of knowing others and being known by them. We build a community of friends and family who are ready to step in the moment we need a helping hand. We have a crew at the ready to celebrate big wins, or just try out the newest Zelda game with. So let's embrace the power of slowing down and bring hope to the lonely hearts around us.

GOD, HELP ME SEE THE LONELINESS AROUND ME

AND BE A SOURCE OF GENUINE LOVE AND HOPE. AMEN.

THE POWER OF GENEROSITY

A generous person will prosper; whoever
refreshes others will be refreshed.

PROVERBS 11:25 NIV

One time, I was at the Atlanta airport, craving some Chick-fil-A goodness. As I walked toward my chicken biscuit, hash browns, *and* chicken minis (yes, I order two entrees), something magical caught my attention. A man was playing the piano in the middle of the terminal, pouring his heart into the music. People were rushing by, not noticing. Normally, I would take my food and go, but I couldn't resist the urge to sit and listen.

I was captivated by the life-giving tunes that flowed from this man's fingertips. He was playing with everything he had, smiling, swaying. But here's the thing: no one seemed to appreciate his talent. So I wanted to make a difference. I approached the piano player, introduced myself, and asked if I could give him a tip. He said his name was Tonee, and he gave me his Cash App info.

Then it hit me. I wanted the Instafamilia to join in on the blessing. I posted on Instagram, rallying my followers to leave Tonee a generous tip. By the time I landed, the tip had multiplied from my initial fifty dollars to more than fifty *thousand* dollars. That's a life-changing amount of money!

Did you know that when we are generous, our brains actually produce more of the hormones that make us feel happy? It's true! We are designed to bring hope to others, and it's not just good for them but for our own well-being too.

When I called Tonee and told him the news, he was overwhelmed with gratitude. You see, Tonee was battling serious health issues, and the money not only helped him financially but also lifted his spirits and restored his hope. And then something else happened. Tonee and I started talking regularly, sharing life, dreams, and laughter. Our friendship became a source of joy and hope for both of us.

See, generosity is not just about the act itself but the ripple effect it creates.

So my challenge to you is this: look for opportunities to be generous. It doesn't have to involve money. You could be generous with a kind word, a helping hand, or a simple act of compassion. Let's bring hope to those around us and experience the joy that comes with giving.

GOD, HELP ME BE AWARE OF THE NEEDS OF OTHERS
AND GIVE FREELY FROM MY HEART. AMEN.

LOVE FROM UP CLOSE

So now I am giving you a new commandment:
Love each other. Just as I have loved
you, you should love each other.
JOHN 13:34

Amigos, I've been a speaker for a long time. I've talked with all kinds of Christians about all kinds of topics. But there's one thing I hear over and over that is oh-so cringe: "I can just love them from afar." People usually say this as a way to not have to love people they disagree with or they find icky.

Fam, we are supposed to be like Jesus. And that is *not* what Jesus did. You know, there's this incredible story about Jesus and ten lepers that reminds us of the power of getting close to people, even when others may be disgusted or afraid.

Picture this: Jesus was walking through a village when He ran into ten lepers. Now, lepers were considered outcasts in those days because their skin disease—a bacteria that could cause sores, bumps, and red patches—was contagious. People were scared of them and would keep their distance. But not Jesus. He saw beyond their disease.

Instead of turning away, Jesus approached them with compassion. He wasn't afraid to get close, even though others might have been. He touched them and spoke words of healing, and they were miraculously cleansed.

Jesus taught us an important lesson that day about embracing others with love. He showed us that no one should be left feeling unaccepted or unloved. Jesus knew that sometimes the people who are considered the least important or most marginalized are the ones who need our love and compassion the most.

I firmly believe that we should all have friends from different walks of life, people who others shy away from. Refugees from another country. People with disabilities. Families that look different from ours. Kids who bring their home troubles to school and act out or get in a lot of fights. Because here's the thing: the person matters more than any issue or disagreement. Jesus didn't love from a distance—He invited everyone to be His friend, especially those who were marginalized. He didn't label them as an issue—He saw them as valuable human beings worthy of love and friendship.

See, when people are seen as issues and not as human beings, it becomes easy to devalue them. But we don't have to compromise our beliefs or change our worldview to become friends with someone. In fact, by opening our hearts and befriending others, we might just change the world.

So here's my challenge to you, amigos. Let's choose to lead with love and bring hope to all. Let's seek friendships that overcome our differences. Let's be there for one another, no matter what.

GOD, THANK YOU FOR SHOWING ME THE POWER OF LOVE

THROUGH JESUS. MAY I ALWAYS SEE PEOPLE AS INDIVIDUALS, NOT ISSUES, AND HELP BRING JOY TO THE WORLD. AMEN.

HOPE AT THE AIRPORT FOOD COURT

In the same way, let your good deeds shine out for all to see, so that everyone will praise your heavenly Father.

MATTHEW 5:16

Ever since I experienced the first Instafamilia fundraiser, there's been something about traveling that makes me think, *We could change that person's life. Or that person's life. Or that person's life.*

Picture this, my friends: another layover in Atlanta, a bustling airport, people rushing all around. And in the middle of it all, a group of hardworking folks cleaning tables and picking up trash at the food court. They were doing their thing, making everything squeaky clean. In that moment, I thought about how they often go unnoticed. And I decided to change that.

I walked up to this guy named Brandon. He had a big smile on his face while wiping down tables. So I struck up a conversation, and guess what? He told me that his joy came from God, who woke him up that morning. But there was more to his story. He'd lost his mom a while back, and now he was taking care of his baby sister all by himself. Talk about responsibility!

Then I met Phyllis, and when I asked her how she was doing, she beamed and said, "I'm blessed!" She told me she was working hard to save enough money to move to a safer, more permanent home. Little did she know how blessed she was about to be.

And there was Josh. He had a young daughter at home and was managing the three-person cleaning crew. It was just him, Brandon, and Phyllis holding it down.

I had an idea. I reached out to my Instafamilia, and together, we set out to spread some love and kindness. We wanted to make these hardworking peeps feel seen and appreciated. So we started collecting donations like crazy!

After forty-five minutes, it was time to share the incredible news. I gathered Brandon, Phyllis, and Josh and spilled the beans. I told them that the Instafamilia had come together and pooled our resources. Each of them was going to get a BIG tip that would go a long way in helping Brandon care for his little sister, Phyllis move to a safer home, and Josh provide for his young daughter.

But this act of kindness wasn't just about the money. It was about showing these hardworking souls, these people who were ignored by thousands of other people a day, that they were seen and appreciated. It was like a little spark of hope in their lives, reminding them that they were not alone.

GOD, THANK YOU FOR REMINDING ME
OF THE POWER OF SIMPLE ACTS OF KINDNESS.
HELP ME BE AWARE OF THE PEOPLE AROUND ME
WHO COULD USE SOME ENCOURAGEMENT. AMEN.

UNEXPECTED LOVE

Do everything with love.

I CORINTHIANS 16:14

I have a confession: I *love* Hallmark Christmas movies. I know, I know. They are cheesy and predictable and completely unrealistic. I don't know why I love them so much. And I especially don't know why they make me tear up every single time. If you don't know what I'm talking about, picture this:

The main character comes home for Christmas, pets a cute dog, and looks up to see . . . the love of their life at the other end of the leash. Or the big-city executive comes home to run the family business and rekindles a grade-school romance. There's snow falling gently from the sky, cozy fireplaces, and towns with names like Evergreen or Mistletoe Hollow. Someone always breaks out in song, and we learn that there's more to Christmas than presents.

But do you know the winning main ingredient in every Hallmark Christmas movie? Unexpected love. Yes, it's that moment when the main character encounters a kind stranger or an old friend, and their world changes forever. The power of love shines through, transforming lives in just a few hours.

Now, here's the exciting part: you can make fifteen-second Hallmark movie moments happen for everyone in your life. Every day, we have the chance to make someone else's day a little brighter with small doses of unexpected love. So what does this look like for you?

136

Here are five suggestions:

1. *Smile.* Flash your pearly whites at someone who may be having a tough day. A smile can light up their world and remind them that they are not alone.
2. *Compliment.* Give a quick shout-out to a friend or classmate. Tell them they are awesome, their outfit is awesome, or they have an amazing sense of humor. It'll make their day!
3. *Hold the door.* When you see someone approaching a door, hold it open with a friendly "After you!" It's a small gesture that shows you care.
4. *Share a treat.* Surprise someone with a small snack or some candy. Offer them a piece of your favorite gum or a yummy chocolate bar. Sweetness spreads faster than gossip!
5. *Write a note.* Jot down a quick note of appreciation and slip it into a friend's locker or backpack. Let them know you're grateful for their friendship.

When we show love to others, we reflect the love that Jesus showed us. He loved the outcasts, the forgotten, and the lonely. His love changed lives, and we can follow His example.

So let's sprinkle some unexpected love into the lives of those around us. Each day, find someone to bless with a fifteen-second dose of love. Be intentional, be creative, and watch their faces light up with joy.

GOD, THANK YOU FOR YOUR LOVE
THAT KNOWS NO BOUNDS. AMEN.

MLK JR.'S GIFTED DREAM

The LORD is good to everyone. He showers
compassion on all his creation.
PSALM 145:9

It was Martin Luther King, Jr. Day, and I found myself craving some delicious Waffle House goodness. If you don't know, Waffle House is a staple here in the South. I just had to get me some hot, fluffy waffles and sizzling, crisp bacon. As I drove there, I found myself thinking about how I could honor Dr. King and his dream for a world of friendship and freedom.

Suddenly, I had an idea. What if I could make some dreams come true? What if I could bring someone an opportunity that seemed out of reach? Or maybe I could give someone a break from disappointment or heartache. Excited to see what God would do, I stepped into the best-smelling place on earth.

Inside, you'll never guess the name of the server who greeted me. Hope. Her name was HOPE! God is so cool. Working alongside Hope were Stacey and Nicole. I asked each of them, "What's your dream?"

Stacey dreamed of owning an RV and retiring. Nicole dreamed of having a home she could call her own and supporting her child through college. Hope dreamed of buying a house where her children could flourish.

I finished my meal—¡delicioso!—paid the check, and left. But I didn't stop there. No way! I drove across the street to Walmart in search of more dreamers. There I met Melinda, who dreamed of seeing Dubai and Amsterdam. And I met Michael, who dreamed of becoming a graphic designer.

But dreams without action are like waffles without syrup—they are not going to get anyone what they want most. So I rallied the Instafamilia to turn these dreams into reality. With each passing hour, donations poured in.

In just twenty-four hours, the Instafamilia raised enough funds to gift Hope, Stacey, Nicole, Melinda, and Michael a staggering $20,000 each! When I went back the next day to share the news, their eyes widened with disbelief, and tears of joy painted their faces.

MLK Jr.'s dream was muy grande—it was a vision for equality, justice, and love for the billions of people who live on this planet. But you don't get to a billion without counting one by one, human by human. Each person has dreams, and we each have opportunities to support others' dreams and keep hope growing, one by one, human by human.

So think about the dreams of your friends, family, and classmates. Does someone dream of becoming a musician? Offer to listen to their songs. Is there a friend who dreams of starting a business? Offer to help them brainstorm ideas. Is there a classmate who dreams of becoming a writer? Offer to read and give feedback on their stories.

Even these small acts of kindness and support can make a big impact on someone's journey to fulfilling their dreams. Let's be dream-builders like Dr. King.

GOD, PLEASE OPEN MY EYES

TO THE DREAMS OF OTHERS. HELP ME SEE WAYS TO SUPPORT THEIR HOPES. AMEN.

WHO SEES YOU?

O Lord, you have examined my heart and know everything about me. You know when I sit down or stand up. You know my thoughts even when I'm far away.

PSALM 139:1–2

I had a huge, important day in my life—the launch of my newest book. A book about really seeing people. It was a big deal, amigos! But guess what? My daughters couldn't be there. My parents couldn't make the trip either. And I felt . . . a little bummed.

But here's the beautiful twist: my amazing wife, Heather, pulled off an epic surprise. She saw how important this book launch was to me. She saw what I was feeling, what I needed. So she secretly flew in our best friends all the way from California. "I can't believe you're here!" I shouted as I threw my arms around them when they arrived. I'm telling you, I was a wreck! I got seen, and it truly changed my world.

I've spent a lot of time learning how to see people. You know, like, really see them. Their needs, their struggles, their dreams. If you want to bring real hope to people, it's important to look beyond the surface, past the Instagram filters, and into the depths of their hearts.

But sometimes I focus so much on seeing others that I forget I also need to be seen. We all long to be known and loved, right down to our messy, imperfect cores. And that's exactly what happened to me that day. I felt seen, loved, and celebrated by those who knew me best.

It reminded me of how our heavenly Father sees us. He knows us inside out, from our silliest secrets to our deepest fears. Nothing is hidden from Him. He sees our smiles and our tears. He sees our victories and our struggles. And you know what? He loves us unconditionally.

So here's the deal, amigos. Take a moment to really think about those around you. Look beyond the surface. See your friends, family, and even strangers with eyes of kindness and understanding. But don't forget that you, too, deserve to be seen and loved. And that you already *are* seen and loved by the God who created the stars in the sky and the freckles on your face. You are given infinite hope by the God who sent Jesus to defeat death!

Keep your eyes open, be a good listener, and spread a little of that hope to those around you. But remember to share your wants, needs, hopes, and dreams with others too.

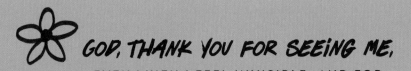

GOD, THANK YOU FOR SEEING ME, EVEN WHEN I FEEL INVISIBLE, AND FOR REMINDING ME THAT I AM LOVED BY YOU. HELP ME SEE OTHERS WITH LOVE AND COMPASSION, JUST AS YOU SEE ME. AMEN.

A RAY OF HOPE AT THE PLUMAS COUNTY FAIR

The LORD is my strength and shield. I trust him with
all my heart. He helps me, and my heart is filled
with joy. I burst out in songs of thanksgiving.

PSALM 28:7

It was August 2021, and Northern California was on fire. The town of Greenville in Plumas County was completely destroyed. One thousand buildings flattened. Five hundred thousand acres scorched. But even in the face of such destruction, the spirit of the community shone bright. They decided to carry on with their annual county fair. What?! In the midst of chaos, they chose hope.

Here's where the story gets even more incredible. I heard about a group of sixty kids from a local 4-H club who were planning to show and sell animals at the fair's livestock auction. Each of these kids had been through unimaginable loss. One girl, Jewel, had fled to safety with her family as their home was overtaken by the fire. She must have been terrified, wondering, *What will happen to us now? Where will we live?* But even in this moment of fear, she was brave enough

142

to rush to the barn and save her goat, Forrest Gump. She held him inside their car as they drove to safety.

Jewel wasn't the only one who'd acted heroically. Kylie had also managed to save her goat while her home burned down, and her brothers Jacob and Holden rescued their steers when their barn burned down. These kids had faced so much, yet they remained unshaken in their determination and love for these animals they had cared for all year long.

For them, agriculture was more than a hobby—it was their way of life.

I knew I couldn't give these kids their houses back, but I *could* find a way to help with the livestock auction. So I reached out to my amazing Instafamilia. I wanted to give these kids a boost, to buy their animals for the highest prices possible . . . but I also didn't have any need (or room) for the animals themselves. So I raised the amount of money they were hoping to get for their animals as a donation. That way, a little pressure was taken off. They could sell their animals for any price and still come out on top.

Guess what? The Instafamilia came through in a big way! We were able to let these resilient young farmers know that they were not alone. Their community—and people from all around the world—saw them and were standing by their side. They learned how much we cared about what they were going through. Cared about their pain. Cared about their dreams. Cared about their future. We wanted them to know that that even in the darkest of times, there is always a ray of hope.

GOD, THANK YOU FOR THE RAY OF HOPE
YOU BROUGHT TO THE PLUMAS COUNTY FAIR. AMEN.

THE LITTLE RED WAGON

And don't forget to do good and to share with those in need. These are the sacrifices that please God.

HEBREWS 13:16

When Zach Bonner was just six years old, his community of Tampa Bay, Florida, was prepared for Hurricane Charley to hit hard. They stocked up on extra supplies like water, knowing that their faucets might not be working for a while. Then they held their breath and waited, until . . . nothing. The hurricane didn't hit Tampa Bay. But it *did* create massive damage to some cities just to the south. Many families had their houses destroyed and hope washed away.

But you know what Zach did? He decided to take action. He loaded up his red toy wagon with water bottles that his family no longer needed and began walking around his neighborhood, asking others to donate their supplies as well. He loaded up that wagon dozens of times! And over the next four months, Zach collected twenty-seven pickup trucks full of supplies for the hurricane victims in need.

Zach's efforts didn't stop there. His compassion for others continued to grow, and he founded an organization called Little Red Wagon when he was seven. This amazing organization focused on helping unhoused communities across the country. Zach traveled from city to city, sharing love, hope, and essential supplies with those in need. He became a light of hope for the unhoused, reminding them that they are seen, valued, and worthy of love.

Amigos, you don't need a little red wagon or lots of money to spread hope. It's about using what you do have and sharing it with others.

You can start by reaching out to a friend who might be feeling down and offering them a listening ear. You can donate some of your clothes or toys to a local shelter. You can even organize a small fundraiser, like a lemonade stand, to raise money for a cause you care about. Remember, every act of love and generosity has the power to make a difference.

So let's spread hope like wildfire, knowing that we—with our big hearts—have the power to make a positive impact in the lives of others. ¡Vamos a hacer una diferencia, mis amigos! (Let's make a difference, my friends!)

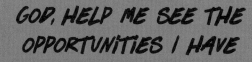

GOD, HELP ME SEE THE OPPORTUNITIES I HAVE

TO BE GENEROUS AND LOVING TOWARD OTHERS. MAY I BE LIKE A LITTLE RED WAGON, CARRYING HOPE AND KINDNESS WHEREVER I GO. AMEN.

UNITED YOUNG DIFFERENCE MAKERS

Don't let anyone think less of you because you are young.
Be an example to all believers in what you say, in the
way you live, in your love, your faith, and your purity.

1 TIMOTHY 4:12

raig Kielburger was twelve years old when he read a newspaper article about a young boy named Iqbal who was forced into child labor. Iqbal had been sold to a carpet factory in Pakistan when he was only four so his parents could afford to take care of his older siblings. Iqbal worked fourteen-hour days, six days a week, tying the tiny knots that make expensive Pakistani rugs. But Iqbal wasn't unique. Craig learned this happened to kids all over the world.

When he learned about how kids like Iqbal were suffering, Craig's corazón (heart) broke. So Craig and ten of his classmates decided to start an advocacy group at school. They met to talk about the issue of child labor and come up with ways they could make a difference.

One idea was to collect signatures on a petition to free a child laborer in India. Craig and his friends were able to get three thousand signatures! They sent the petition to the prime minister of India himself. After that, Craig's organization got so much attention, he raised $150,000 to help free children around the world. With the help of his parents, he founded Free the Children, a movement to empower young people to fight for the rights of children around the world. And let me tell you, their impact was HUGE!

Free the Children worked with local community members to build schools like Kisaruni Secondary School in the Maasai Mara region of Kenya, providing education to girls from Indigenous communities. They installed water systems that provided clean and accessible water to households in rural communities like the Chimborazo province of Ecuador. They built health clinics and provided medical supplies, equipment, and training in places like Sierra Leone, where the people have been impacted by the Ebola outbreak. Craig and his amigos showed the world what it looks like to be hope builders!

But Craig's work didn't stop there. As he grew older, he continued to spread hope and make a difference. Free the Children became WE Charity. Along with building schools and health clinics and providing clean water, WE focuses on getting kids involved in changing the world.

Craig Kielburger's story is a reminder that we all have the power to change the world. Just like Craig, we can be hope builders in our own communities, collecting books for Little Free Libraries, filling backpacks for kids in need, or collecting coats and socks and blankets for those who are sleeping outside when the weather turns cold. We can make a difference and spread hope—one act of kindness at a time.

GOD, PLEASE FILL MY HEART
WITH COMPASSION AND GIVE ME THE COURAGE TO TAKE ACTION. AMEN.

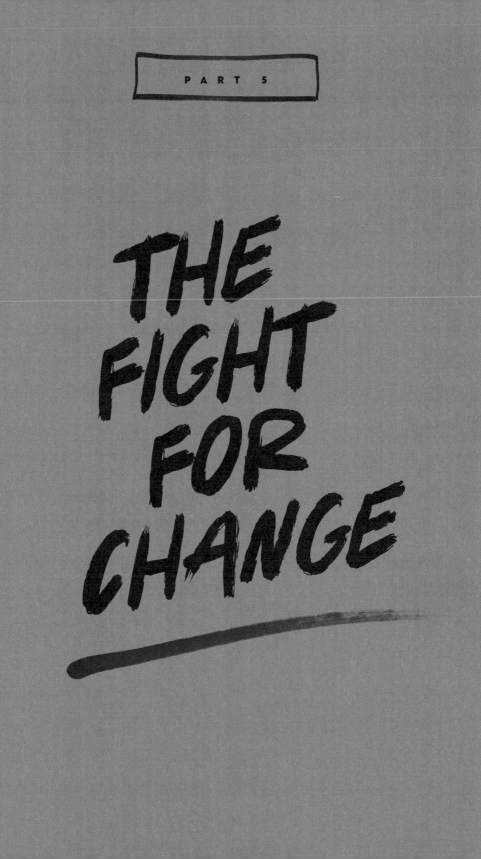

PART 5

THE FIGHT FOR CHANGE

UNAFRAID DREAMERS

I pray that God, the source of hope, will fill you
completely with joy and peace because you trust
in him. Then you will overflow with confident
hope through the power of the Holy Spirit.

ROMANS 15:13

I've met and talked with a lot of hope-filled world changers in my life, but Bambadjan Bamba has to be one of my favorites. And not just because his name is really fun to say. Bambadjan Bamba, now a famous actor, faced unbelievable challenges growing up, but he never gave up hope for himself or for others.

Bambadjan was born in Africa, in the Ivory Coast. Life was like a dream in the country of green mountains, blue ocean, and elephants. His family vacationed at fancy hotels and ice-skated at Christmastime. But then everything changed. The Ivory Coast became unsafe, and his family had to leave. They sought safety in America.

Bambadjan was ten years old when he and his family arrived in the Bronx, part of New York City. America was a different world for Bambadjan. He couldn't speak English, and he was bullied and beaten up, just because he was different.

As soon as they arrived in America, Bambadjan's parents filed government papers to get permission to live and work in the country.

Year after year, they waited for approval . . . and eight years later, they *still* hadn't gotten it. And here's the kicker: Bambadjan was now an adult. He needed his own paperwork. But if he tried to get his own documents, he would be immediately sent back to the Ivory Coast because he'd already lived in the United States for eight years. Suddenly, Bambadjan became an *un*documented adult, illegal in his own home.

Then something incredible happened. Adults who had been brought to America as kids, just like Bambadjan, stood up and made their voices heard. They called themselves "undocumented and unafraid," speaking up for their rights. Their bravery caught the attention of President Barack Obama, who signed a law that gave nearly one million people protection from being kicked out of the country and permission to work and pay taxes. The law is called DACA: Deferred Action for Childhood Arrivals, and it allowed people like Bambadjan to chase their dreams!

Bambadjan seized this opportunity and pursued his passion for acting. He worked hard, landed roles in TV shows, and even appeared in blockbuster movies like *Black Panther*. In 2017, when DACA was set to expire, he boldly used his platform to identify himself as undocumented in the hopes that it would inspire other influential people to advocate for DACA. What a hero!

You have the power to make a difference too. The Bible says that because you are connected to God, you will *overflow* with confident hope. The kind of hope you need to raise your voice, call out unfairness, and support others who are fighting for change!

GOD, HELP ME SEE THAT CHANGE IS POSSIBLE, AND GIVE ME THE COURAGE TO FIGHT FOR JUSTICE. AMEN.

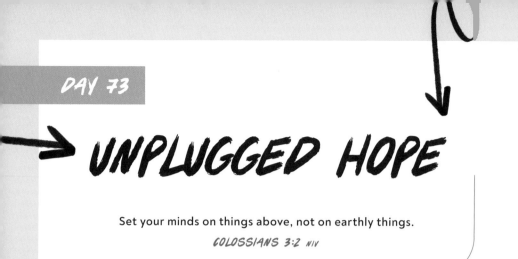

UNPLUGGED HOPE

Set your minds on things above, not on earthly things.
COLOSSIANS 3:2 NIV

Recently, I took this crazy seven-week break from all social media. That included Instagram, where I usually spend hours scrolling and sharing. Actually, I took a seven-week break from my whole phone.

I needed space from the constant noise, you know? The pressure to impress and get those virtual high fives. So I unplugged and dived into the real world. And guess what? It felt like a breath of fresh air. I felt lighter, more hopeful. And it allowed me to think about all the ways I wanted to change the world—starting with everyone spending a little less time scrolling and a little more time strolling.

Okay, that was cheesy. But you get what I'm saying. The human brain was not made to consume the amount of information we consume on a daily basis. There's so much broken in the world that when we have access to ALL the brokenness at once, we get kind of paralyzed.

When I didn't have constant access to my phone, I learned to soak up the moment instead of living for the likes. And in one of those moments, something truly magical happened: I had the opportunity to rescue a baby hummingbird.

I stumbled upon Ruthie (yes, I named her) when she was just a tiny creature, barely the length of my pinky finger. She was fragile and helpless, but her spirit was full of life. I was captivated by the thought of caring for this tiny being.

152

Normally, I would be posting live updates the whole time, going back and forth with hundreds of people in my DMs about how to care for a baby hummingbird, but not this time. It was just me and Ruthie. No distractions, no pressure to perform. It was pure magic, my friends!

Without the urge to document and post about every step, I nurtured Ruthie and watched her grow stronger over three days. I provided her with warmth, shelter, and a nourishing diet of insects. Throughout it all, I cherished the magic in being distraction-free around her.

So, my awesome amigos, I challenge you to also take a break from the digital noise sometimes. It doesn't have to be seven weeks. It could be one week. Or one day. Or thirty minutes! Figure out the amount of time that's right for you, then step away. Set your mind on something bigger than the screen in your hands, and embrace the incredible now. Know that God is always with you, cheering you on. There's no need to impress anyone. Just be yourself and enjoy the journey.

GOD, THANK YOU FOR REMINDING ME TO SLOW DOWN

AND APPRECIATE THE PRESENT. HELP ME FIND THE BALANCE BETWEEN THE ONLINE WORLD AND REAL-LIFE CONNECTIONS THAT FILL ME WITH HOPE. AMEN.

BE BRAVE; BE HOPEFUL

This is my command—be strong and courageous!
Do not be afraid or discouraged. For the LORD
your God is with you wherever you go.

JOSHUA 1:9

Let me introduce you to Malala Yousafzai, this brave chica who fought for change and brought hope to women and girls all around the world. Imagine being a young girl around your age living in a place where girls were told they couldn't go to school or be anything other than a wife and mother when they grew up. Oh boy, Malala wasn't having any of that!

Malala believed in the power of education for every girl. Threats against girls going to school didn't keep her at home. She also wrote blogs detailing her experiences and advocating for girls' education. Unfortunately, this made her a target for those who didn't agree. In 2012, while on her way home from school, she was shot by the Taliban. But Malala didn't let even that stop her! Instead, she rose even stronger and more determined to fight for girls' education.

After surviving the attack, she started the Malala Fund, an organization that helps girls all over the world go to school. Another supercool thing she did was create the Gulmakai Network. It's like a team of education heroes in different countries, like Afghanistan,

Nigeria, Pakistan, and Lebanon. They build schools, train teachers, and make sure girls get a chance to learn. How cool is that?

Malala's not just about building schools though. Her voice and passion have made governments and people pay attention to girls' education. Because of Malala, they are making new rules and realizing how important it is for girls to have a chance to learn and follow their dreams.

Here's the deal, fam: fighting for change can be *hard* and even really scary. But it can also make a BIG difference and can cause cannonball-size ripples of hope through the world. Maybe there's something you're super passionate about—like stopping bullying, planting more trees, or providing shoes to kids in developing countries. Well, guess what? You have the power to create change! Raise your voice, share your ideas, and take action!

Let's take a moment to reflect on God's Word. The earlier verse from the book of Joshua reminds us to be strong and courageous, knowing that God is with us every step of the way. God is with you when you fight for change, which means His infinite hope is with you too. He's got our backs, my friends!

So don't be afraid to stand up for what's right, fight for change, and be a shining beacon of hope in your world. Together, we can create a place filled with kindness, love, and endless possibilities.

GOD, HELP ME BE JUST AS COURAGEOUS AND PASSIONATE

AS MALALA YOUSAFZAI. SHOW ME
HOW I CAN SPREAD RIPPLES OF HOPE
THROUGH MY WORLD. AMEN.

THE HOPE OF BLACK AUNTIES

When she speaks, her words are wise, and
she gives instructions with kindness.

PROVERBS 31:26

Have you ever met a Black auntie? At our church, we have five: Sharon, Melinda, Sarah, Carine, and Candace. They are like superheroes in our community, spreading love, wisdom, and hope everywhere they go. They are also some of the most joyful, hilarious women you will ever meet—I dare you not to laugh when you start talking with them!

Of course, none of these incredible women are *my* aunts, but they are aunts to some really lucky kids. So why do we all call them Black aunties? Well, because they *act* like everyone's aunts. They are the mentors, the people kids can go to when they need to talk to an adult but can't or don't want to talk to their parents. They are also honest when they need to be. As Sarah says, "You ain't going out there looking [or acting] some kinda way!" Seriously. They love us all too much to let us embarrass ourselves or others.

Bottom line: you're going to know that you are seen and *adored* when you're in the presence of a Black auntie.

But Black aunties also carry a heavy burden. In spaces like our church, where they are surrounded by mostly White friends, they get asked a lot of questions. Questions like "Can I touch your hair?" or "Why did the guy who plays Genie in *Aladdin* slap the guy who voices Marty in *Madagascar* during an awards show?" So whenever something that happens within the Black community makes headlines, they have to send up a prayer: "Dear Lord, I need to show up with strength tomorrow." Strength to answer those questions with grace. Strength to educate their friends and keep fighting for change. Strength to be leaders and spread joy. It's a heavy burden, my friends.

Thankfully, these aunties don't have to do this work all on their own. We can honor and support the aunties in our communities—or the auntie-like people old and young, men and women—who lift the community up, spread hope, and carry pain. Here's how:

1. *Say "thank you."* This is especially important when they take the time to answer one of your questions.
2. *Share what you learn.* That's one less person the auntie has to educate and one excellent way you can help in the fight for change!
3. *Be a mentor.* Start acting like an auntie to the younger kids in your community. Show up with kindness, patience, and honesty, and be a person who brings joy into their lives.

Together with the incredible aunties surrounding us, we can make our communities brighter and more loving places.

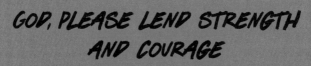

GOD, PLEASE LEND STRENGTH AND COURAGE

TO THE PEOPLE IN MY LIFE WHO ARE ALWAYS THERE TO SUPPORT, LOVE, AND EDUCATE ME. AMEN.

HOPE FOR HOMETOWNS

> Faith means being sure of the things we hope for. And faith means knowing that something is real even if we do not see it.
>
> *HEBREWS 11:1 ICB*

Michael Tubbs is a true inspiration in fighting for change. Michael grew up in Stockton, California, where he faced a lot of challenges. His mom had him as a teenager, and his dad spent most of his life in prison. But something special happened in Michael's church. He discovered hope, and it ignited a fire within him. He started preaching at a young age, finding the courage and confidence to be a leader in his community.

While Michael was away at college, tragedy struck when his cousin was murdered back home in Stockton. It was a wake-up call for Michael. He realized that he couldn't turn a blind eye to the struggles his community faced. Against the advice of many, he returned to Stockton. He knew his city needed him.

A few years later, when Michael was twenty-six years old, he became the mayor of Stockton—the *youngest* mayor they had ever had. Under his leadership, incredible things happened. Stockton was recognized as an All-America City, crime rates dropped, and the city's finances improved.

Amigos, I don't think I can overstate what a HUGE change that was. Stockton had been a city in trouble. Many families couldn't afford food and housing. Kids were dropping out of school. People didn't feel safe leaving their homes or cars unlocked because of all the crime. But Michael's hope burned bright. He believed that change was possible, even when others doubted it. Years later, he would name his daughter Nehemiah, after a biblical figure who had a similar deep burden and hope for his hometown.

In a world where many lose hope, Michael's perseverance shines through. When I talked to Michael, I was so blown away by the power we each have to create change, even when faced with overwhelming challenges—and even when we have to face those challenges early in life. Just like when an adult asks you to clean up a mess, Michael saw the mess in his community—and it was a BIG mess—and chose to take action.

Hope is a powerful force. Let it guide you as you bring change—big or small—to your own communities. Keep shining bright, and never lose sight of the impact you can make.

GOD, THANK YOU FOR INSPIRING LEADERS
WHO BRING HOPE TO THEIR COMMUNITIES. AMEN.

HOPE FOR AMERICA

> Blessed is the nation whose God is the Lord. Happy
> are the people He has chosen for His own.
>
> *PSALM 33:12 NLV*

I love America. I love fireworks. I love cookouts. I love the purple mountain majesties. I love everything from sea to shining sea! And because of the deep love I have for my country, I've taken it upon myself to learn as much as I can about its complicated history. After all, you can't truly love something unless you know and love all of it—good, bad, and ugly.

You see, when I hear that America began in 1776, I can't help but think, *Now, wait a minute. There were people here long before that.* Maybe the version of America we know today started in 1776, but that ignores centuries of rich history that happened right here on the land where our homes, our businesses, and our Starbucks coffee shops sit today.

Indigenous Americans were left out of our society for a super-long time. Did you know it wasn't until 1920 that they even became citizens? And here's another uncomfortable fact: our young country is also one of the wealthiest . . . for an ugly reason. America was able to gain wealth and power so quickly because some of the first folks who came here from Europe took land without buying it. And then they enslaved people and made them work the land for free. We can all agree that was not right. It's a part of our history that we can't ignore.

But do we throw in the towel? Give up hope on this great nation? No way!

Despite all the dark stuff, I still believe America is an amazing country. It's full of hope, freedom, and a whole lot of different people. Plus, we've come a long way. We abolished slavery, fought for civil rights, and continue to strive for a fairer and more inclusive society. Today we recognize and celebrate the contributions and resilience of Indigenous communities.

If we want hope for America, we have to let go of the idea that our history is some kind of fairy tale. It's gonna be uncomfortable, but that's life, my friends. Sometimes we gotta face the uncomfortable.

Just like Adam and Eve's sin led to a broken relationship with God, America has the stain of injustice and oppression. But just as God provided a way for redemption and reconciliation through Jesus, America can find healing and restoration through Him too!

Fam, we can love America and still hope to make it better. Take the time to learn about our nation's history, including the struggles and triumphs of different communities. Believe in a brighter future, step by step. A future where we learn from the past, have tough conversations, and work together to make America even better. We can be a generation that brings positive change, spreading hope and understanding.

GOD, THANKS FOR AMERICA,

THIS LAND OF HOPE AND DREAMS. HELP US FACE THE TRUTH OF OUR HISTORY, AND SHOW ME HOW TO MAKE EVERYONE FEEL SEEN AND LOVED. AMEN.

THE GREEN REVOLUTION 2.0

> I tell you the truth, if you had faith even as small as a mustard seed, you could say to this mountain, "Move from here to there," and it would move. Nothing would be impossible.
>
> *MATTHEW 17:20*

One thing that connects every human around the world is the need for food. No matter where you live, what you look like, or what you believe, you need to eat. Preferably three healthy meals a day. But that's not possible for a lot of people. Big, complicated problems like the economy and climate and politics can make it hard for people to find enough food. And the problem started getting worse in 2018.

From 2018 to 2023, the number of people who really can't get enough food to live went from 80 million to nearly 350 million.

BUT WAIT. I'm not telling you this to make you feel hopeless. I'm telling you this because this is a problem we've faced before—and solved!

In the 1950s and 1960s, one in three people were going to bed with empty bellies. But instead of feeling defeated, brilliant minds all around the world developed a secret weapon: a tiny seed of hope that grew into fields and fields of crops.

One of those brilliant minds belonged to Norman Borlaug. He

162

was a rock star in the world of agriculture. And he believed that if he and others put their heads together, they could conquer the mountain of hunger. And conquer they did! Norman and his team started what we now call the Green Revolution. Norman rolled up his sleeves, dug his hands into the dirt, and figured out how to grow *a lot* more food.

He helped make new and better ways to water crops *and* came up with seeds that could fight off crop-killing diseases. As the years went by, these efforts bore fruit—literally! Food production skyrocketed, and millions of people were fed who would have otherwise gone hungry. The mountain of hunger began to crumble before their very eyes.

You see, my friends, that's the power of hope. It can transform deserts into oases and barren lands into bountiful fields. The Green Revolution taught us that even when things seem impossible, hope gives us the courage to dream big and take action.

But the Green Revolution isn't just a story from the past. It's a reminder for us all today. You might look at the world's problems and think they are too big for you, like an insurmountable mountain. But remember, faith as small as a mustard seed can move mountains!

Maybe you're passionate about protecting our environment, fighting for justice, or helping those in need. Or maybe you'll start the second Green Revolution! Whatever it is, hold on to that seed of faith. Believe that with God's help and your willingness to take action, nothing is impossible. Go out there and be the difference maker you were created to be!

GOD, HELP ME SEE THE MOUNTAINS IN MY OWN LIFE

AND THE WORLD AROUND ME AS OPPORTUNITIES FOR CHANGE. AMEN.

IS THE WORLD FALLING APART?

So let's not get tired of doing what is good.
At just the right time we will reap a harvest
of blessing if we don't give up.

GALATIANS 6:9

Recently, I took seven weeks off from social media. If you don't think that sounds hard, let me put it this way: that's as long as most summer breaks from school. Or almost as long as the time between Halloween and Christmas. In other words, it was a long break . . . but it was also great. My brain and body relaxed as I separated myself from the world's struggles and other people's worries, angers, and insecurities.

But one thing I was surprised by when I logged back on to social media was that people were *still* screaming about how the world was falling apart. And it made me think, *Maybe the world has always been falling apart. Maybe the world always* will be *falling apart.*

Have you ever felt overwhelmed by all the problems in the world? We know this is not the way God meant for the world to be. But ever since the first humans, Adam and Eve, disobeyed God and ate the fruit from the Tree of Knowledge of Good and Evil, the world has not stuck to God's perfect design.

The truth is, we live in a broken world, and it can be easy to lose hope. But I've got good news for you: even in this broken world, you have the power to make a difference. When you love others, care for the earth and its creatures, and care about justice and equality, you are bringing the world closer to the way God made it.

In Scripture, we find hope to fight for change every day. The apostle Paul encourages us, through his letter to the Galatians, to never get tired of doing what is good.

How do we do these good deeds? It might be as simple as sharing that thing with your sibling that they are always trying to borrow, sending an encouraging message to a friend, or offering to help around the house.

You can fight for change by taking care of our planet. Maybe it's picking up litter at the park or volunteering at a local charity. Plant a tree, conserve energy by turning off the lights before you leave the house, or participate in a community cleanup. Small actions like these add up and contribute to a more perfect world.

Change can start with you. Change can start today. And the best part is, your small acts of kindness and compassion will inspire others to follow your example.

So don't let the brokenness of the world discourage you. Instead, let it ignite a fire within you to never get tired of doing good.

GOD, THANK YOU FOR REMINDING ME

THAT I HAVE THE POWER TO MAKE THE WORLD A MORE PERFECT PLACE. HELP ME SEE THE NEEDS AROUND ME EVERY DAY, AND GIVE ME THE COURAGE TO TAKE ACTION. AMEN.

ACCESS TO CLEAN WATER

And if you give even a cup of cold water to one of the least of my followers, you will surely be rewarded.

MATTHEW 10:42

A few years ago, I traveled to the country of Uganda in Africa. The people, the culture, the food, the land, and the animals were all *incredible*. But not everything about the Ugandans' lives was incredible. They faced some real struggles that I had never even thought about. One of the most significant struggles was the difficulty of getting clean water.

Honestly, lots of people in the United States don't even know why unclean water is so harmful to communities around the world. They are living the sweet life, turning on faucets where drinkable water flows freely. But in Uganda and other countries in Sub-Saharan Africa, dirty water means people get sick a lot and sometimes even die. It also means kids don't have access to private and clean toilets at school. Can you imagine how hard that would be?

And the difficulty doesn't stop there. Often when people can get clean water, they have to carry huge buckets for miles to get it home. These people spend their days searching for something I often take for granted. How unfair is that?

Thankfully, I am not the first person to see this crisis in the world.

A bunch of charities have joined hands to help. Organizations like Water.org, The Water Project, Filter of Hope, and UNICEF's Water, Sanitation, and Hygiene (WASH) programs. These groups build wells and purifying systems that bring clean, life-giving water to communities that need it the most. But they are not just giving people water—they are giving them hope for a better future.

My friend, you have the power to make a difference too. Start by spreading awareness about the clean water crisis. Talk to your friends, your family, and your teachers, and let them know about the challenges faced by millions of people around the world. Ask ten friends for five dollars and use the money to buy a water filter for a family in need through Filter of Hope.

And let's not forget the power of prayer. We can pray for those who are struggling, for the organizations working tirelessly, and for the resources needed to bring clean water to the globe. Prayer is a weapon of hope, and it connects us to the One who can move mountains—and heavy buckets of water.

With each step we take, with each well we dig, with each drop of clean water we provide, we are making a difference. We are writing a story of hope, love, and transformation.

GOD, THANK YOU FOR THE GIFT OF CLEAN WATER.

HELP ME FIGHT FOR CHANGE AND BRING CLEAN WATER TO THOSE WHO NEED IT. AMEN.

FUEL FOR A BRIGHTER FUTURE

Don't be afraid, for I am with you. Don't be discouraged,
for I am your God. I will strengthen you and help you.
I will hold you up with my victorious right hand.

ISAIAH 41:10

During the time of the civil rights movement in Selma, Alabama, Amelia Boynton and her Black neighbors weren't allowed to go places that White people could go. They couldn't go to good schools or get good jobs or even vote to start making changes for their people. But in the midst of fear and uncertainty, God's promise in Isaiah 41:10 rang true: "Don't be afraid, for I am with you."

Amelia decided she'd had enough. She believed in God's strength and, with a heart full of hope, organized peaceful marches. The most famous march happened one Sunday in 1965.

As they approached a bridge, the crowd came face to face with a line of police. In a tragic turn of events that would forever be etched in history as "Bloody Sunday," the police swung batons and released tear gas.

An officer on horseback hit Amelia across the back of her shoulders with his baton. Then he hit her again on the back of her neck. That's when she passed out. A photo of Amelia lying unconscious on the ground was printed on the front page of newspapers all around

the country. And it got the attention of the nation.

Still, they kept their hopes up. Over the next couple of weeks, people all around the nation traveled to Selma, determined to finish the march. Finally, with federal law enforcement marching alongside and protecting them, 25,000 people, including Amelia Boynton, reached Montgomery.

Amelia and her fellow marchers chose not to be discouraged by the challenges they faced. They kept their eyes fixed on God's promise and pressed on. Later that same year, the Voting Rights Act of 1965, which guaranteed equal voting rights for all, was signed.

So my friends, when life feels tough, remember Isaiah 41:10. God is always with you, ready to strengthen and help you. With His strength, you can stand up against injustice, fight for what is right, and bring about positive change in your world.

GOD, THANK YOU FOR YOUR PROMISE

TO BE WITH ME AND STRENGTHEN ME. HELP ME HAVE THE COURAGE AND PERSEVERANCE TO STAND UP FOR JUSTICE AND MAKE A DIFFERENCE IN THE LIVES OF OTHERS. AMEN.

ARE YOU A BUILDER OR A DESTROYER?

> At last the wall was completed to half
> its height around the entire city, for the
> people had worked with enthusiasm.
>
> *NEHEMIAH 4:6*

Humans are drawn to destruction. Don't believe me? Give a toddler a hammer and a fully built LEGO set and see what happens.

Actually, please don't give a toddler a hammer. Or any kind of tool. That could be a little *too* destructive. And dangerous.

But you get my point. As satisfying as it is to build the tallest block tower or cup pyramid or card castle . . . there's just something in us that gets a kick out of knocking it down. It makes no sense.

Hopefully you don't have social media. No, not because you're a kid and—let me bust out my dad voice—"Science says it's bad for your developing brain." That may be true, but I'm pretty sure it can be bad for *any* brain.

So then why do I hope you don't have social media? Well, a lot of reasons, but mostly because the majority of what I see on social media is people yelling about what they are against and what they want to destroy. Because destroying is easier than building. But it isn't nearly as effective. And it's a hope killer.

Now, there are some things that *need* to be destroyed. BIG things like hate. Corruption. Discrimination. Sin. But as important as it is to destroy evil things, it's more *hopeful* to build than destroy.

In the Bible, the book of Nehemiah tells the story of the rebuilding of Jerusalem's walls. The Babylonians had destroyed the city and taken the Israelites into captivity. Finally, the Israelites were back in their homeland, but the city was in ruins.

Now, back in Nehemiah's day, a city wasn't a city unless it had walls to protect it. If the Israelites wanted to return to rebuild Jerusalem, they had to start with the walls.

Everyone helped. Farmers, teachers, craftsmen, and priests all took shifts working. It took a long time. Building something you are for takes more work than destroying something you are against. But instead of ending up with a total mess, you have something to be proud of, something to keep building up with hope. The Bible says the people worked with "enthusiasm." I guarantee the Jews' positive energy of rebuilding that wall felt a million times better than the Babylonians' hatred of destroying it.

I spend a lot of energy destroying the things I am against. And I think that's okay. *As long as* I spend double the amount of energy building things I am for.

You want to stand out in a sea of rage? Find what you're *for*. Then build!

GOD, HELP ME FOCUS LESS ON DESTROYING

THE THINGS I AM AGAINST. SHOW ME WAYS I CAN FIGHT FOR CHANGE AND BUILD THE THINGS I AM FOR. AMEN.

A KALEIDOSCOPE OF EXPERIENCES

Spouting off before listening to the facts
is both shameful and foolish.

PROVERBS 18:13

Have you ever looked through a kaleidoscope? You know, one of those little toys you put up to one eye, tilt toward a light source, and rotate around to see all the different shapes and colors and patterns it makes? It's just one tiny toy, but every way you turn it, you see something different.

Life is kind of like one of those colorful kaleidoscopes, filled with diverse experiences and unique perspectives. And if there's one thing I've learned, it's that we need to open our ears and our hearts to truly understand and support one another.

Have your friends told you about being treated differently than other people? Maybe you've heard about the daily "microaggressions" or racist or sexist words or actions people experience. Things like people being surprised by how well-spoken you are. People being afraid of you because of the way you look. People asking you where you're *really* from. Maybe you've experienced these things yourself.

I want to share something my friend told me. He's friends with a White family at church. They had two biological sons and then adopted two Black sons the same age as their biological sons. When their sons were around thirteen, something changed. The parents noticed how their biological sons and their adopted sons were treated very differently. They told my friend they had no idea how bad racism really was . . . until they saw it firsthand.

My friend turned to me and said one of the most moving things I've ever heard: "Don't wait until the pain knocks on your door to care and fight for change."

You know, it's easy to remain ignorant or turn a blind eye to the struggles of others, especially when they don't directly impact our lives. But that's not what it means to love our neighbor as ourselves. God calls us to step into their shoes, to feel their pain, and to fight for change.

We shouldn't wait until injustice touches us personally to care. No, my friends, we must open our minds and hearts now. We need to be agents of change in the world.

How? It starts with actively seeking opportunities to listen and learn from others. This means engaging in conversations with people who have different backgrounds and experiences than our own. It means reading books with characters who look, believe, and live differently than you.

But it doesn't stop there, my young hope warriors. We must also take action. Small acts of kindness and understanding can create a ripple effect that spreads healing in our world—and hope for change wherever we go.

GOD, THANK YOU FOR REMINDING ME

OF THE POWER OF LISTENING AND BELIEVING THE EXPERIENCES OF OTHERS. EMPOWER ME TO STAND AGAINST INJUSTICE AND TO BE AN AGENT OF CHANGE IN MY COMMUNITY. AMEN.

A BRIGHTER TOMORROW

We can rejoice, too, when we run into problems and trials, for we know that they help us develop endurance. And endurance develops strength of character, and character strengthens our confident hope of salvation.

ROMANS 5:3–4

Have you heard of a man named Nelson Mandela? He was a true hero who fought for justice and equality. And wow, did he keep his hopes up through a *lot* of challenges.

Nelson Mandela was born in a small village in South Africa, where life was tough, especially because of something called apartheid. Apartheid was a system that treated people unfairly just because of their race. Public spaces were divided into White spaces and Black spaces. Black people were only allowed to live in certain communities. They could only marry other Black people. And Black kids were not allowed to receive a quality education. Despite all this, Nelson Mandela put his hope in a South Africa where everyone could live in harmony, regardless of their skin color.

Mandela spoke out against the policies of apartheid and formed a group called the African National Congress that encouraged people to break the unjust laws. All he wanted was fair laws for his people, but Mandela was imprisoned for trying to overthrow the government! Even in the darkest moments, however, Mandela never lost hope.

From prison, he continued writing letters to fellow activists and government officials. He met with South African leaders to brainstorm ideas for a peaceful resolution. Finally, after Nelson Mandela had spent twenty-seven years in prison, South Africans started to see how unfair apartheid was. Mandela was released and immediately got to work trying to end apartheid once and for all.

Four years later, he became the first Black president of South Africa and united a divided nation. Through his leadership and dedication to peace, laws restricting Black people from land ownership were overturned and South Africa began practicing restorative justice—a philosophy focused on how to repair the damage that crimes bring to people and communities. Most significantly, Mandela showed the world the power of the human spirit and the limitless hope we can find in God.

Hope is a powerful force. It empowers us to fight for what is right, to stand up against injustice, and to make a difference in the world around us. We can face challenges—big or small—with the confidence that God's limitless hope is in us, giving us the courage and determination to bring positive change.

GOD, HELP ME ALWAYS KEEP MY HOPES UP,

EVEN WHEN THINGS GET TOUGH. FILL MY HEART WITH YOUR LIMITLESS HOPE SO THAT I CAN BE AN AGENT OF CHANGE IN MY OWN COMMUNITY. AMEN.

SPLASHES OF HOPE

Do not withhold good from those who deserve it when it's in your power to help them.

PROVERBS 3:27

Have you ever heard of the ALS Ice Bucket Challenge? Well, let me tell you, it made quite the splash way back in 2014! The challenge encouraged those who were nominated to be filmed having a bucket of ice water poured on their heads and then nominating others to do the same. All for the purpose of raising awareness—and money—for amyotrophic lateral sclerosis (ALS, or Lou Gehrig's disease).

But it didn't start as a way to raise money for ALS. It started as just a silly challenge to raise awareness for any cause . . . until pro golfer Chris Kennedy challenged his wife's cousin. In the process, he called out the little-known disease that one of his family members was suffering from—ALS. ALS is a pretty rare disease, which is why so many people hadn't heard of it. But it is very serious. It affects people's muscle movements, making it difficult for them to walk, talk, and eventually even eat. But thanks to the video that Chris Kennedy posted, awareness began to spread like wildfire.

People from all walks of life, including celebrities, athletes, and even us regular folks, took part in this unique challenge—and brought hope to millions. Not only did the challenge raise awareness, but it also raised an enormous amount of funds—over $220 million worldwide—to support ALS research aimed at finding a cure. It united us, showing the power we have when we come together for a cause. Through social media shares, videos, and donations, we made a massive impact.

Sometimes all it takes is a little splash of awareness to create a tidal wave of hope. By simply spreading the word about a cause, we can make a difference in the lives of so many. The massive impact of the ALS Ice Bucket Challenge reminds us that our actions, no matter how small, can have an ENORME ripple effect.

So my friends, never underestimate the power of your voice. When you see an opportunity to shine a light on an important issue, take it. Share it with your friends, your family, and your community. Be a voice for those who may not have one. Your voice can bring hope, ignite change, and inspire others to join the cause.

Together we can make a splash in this world and bring hope to those who need it!

Stay cool, stay joyful, and keep making waves of hope.

GOD, THANK YOU FOR REMINDING ME

THAT I HAVE THE POWER TO MAKE A DIFFERENCE. HELP ME BE BOLD IN SPREADING AWARENESS, SHINING A LIGHT ON IMPORTANT ISSUES, AND BRINGING HOPE TO THOSE WHO NEED IT MOST. AMEN.

LITTLE MISS FLINT

Give justice to the poor and the orphan; uphold
the rights of the oppressed and the destitute.
PSALM 82:3

Did you know that not having access to clean, drinkable water isn't just a problem in countries like Uganda? It's a problem right here in America too.

In 2014 the people of Flint, Michigan, were facing a water crisis. The water coming out of the faucets in their homes had lead in it. Lead can be poisonous in large amounts.

The lead in their water was causing kids to have developmental delays and learning disabilities. It was also causing adults to have heart problems and kidney damage. Their water was making them *sick*—and it had been for years. They tried to tell lawmakers, but no one would believe them and fix it. People were getting discouraged and losing hope. But not Mari Copeny, a girl who would soon be given the nickname "Little Miss Flint."

Seven-year-old Mari didn't just sit back and hope for things to get better. No, she took action! She wrote a letter to the president at the time—Barack Obama. When President Obama read Mari's letter, he actually traveled to Flint to meet with Mari and talk about the water crisis!

After that visit, Flint's water crisis had the attention of the nation—and the rest of the world. Mari organized events and even

led a campaign to collect and distribute clean water to those in need. She embodied the spirit of her city: she was strong, courageous, and steadfast, like a hard flint rock. And this determination and resilience earned her the title of Little Miss Flint.

When Mari spoke up and took action, she grew hope in the hearts of people who were feeling hopeless. She showed them that someone cared, that someone was fighting for them—and she wasn't going to give up until real change was made.

Amigos, that's what hope does. It lifts us up. It reminds us that we're not alone. And it gives us the strength to seek justice and fight for people's rights, just like the Bible instructs us to do.

God's love is like a limitless well of hope. When we tap into that well and let it flow through us, we can bring hope to others. Just like Mari did for her community. She became a beacon of hope, inspiring others to join the fight. That's what it looks like to make a real difference!

GOD, HELP ME SEE THE PROBLEMS AROUND ME,
AND GIVE ME THE STRENGTH TO STAND UP AND FIGHT FOR WHAT IS RIGHT. AMEN.

A DELICIOUS PLACE TO LIVE

For we are God's masterpiece. He has created
us anew in Christ Jesus, so we can do the
good things he planned for us long ago.

EPHESIANS 2:10

Omari McQueen is a young hero who saw a documentary about how our choices impact the world and decided to make a difference. This kid's got some serious hope and a heart full of passion!

Omari was just a seven-year-old kid scrolling YouTube when he came across a video about how animals used for food and clothes are kept in very small cages and subjected to painful farming practices. What's more, animal agriculture is messy and can harm the environment. The documentary made Omari sad. He didn't like how our food choices can harm animals and affect the planet we call home. Instead of just feeling sad or overwhelmed, he tapped into his hope for a better world—and his love for cooking!—and took action.

Omari started his own online business, selling delicious vegan dips like beetroot ketchup and sun-dried tomato hummus. Today, he's expanded beyond dips and offers vegan meal kits. His kits include things like vegan tacos, colorful grain bowls packed with vegetables and grains, aromatic curries with a variety of spices and vegetables, and refreshing salads bursting with fresh ingredients.

He turned his hope for a kinder, healthier planet into something tangible and impactful. And you know what? His food is amazing! Omari's business not only brings joy to people's taste buds but also spreads awareness about the treatment of animals, the environment, and the power of our choices.

Omari didn't stop there though. He used his platform to inspire others to join the fight for change. Through social media, interviews, and even writing a book, he's shared his story and encouraged everyone to find their passion and make a difference—just like he did.

When we connect our hopes for the world with our actions, incredible things can happen. It's not just about dreaming or wishing for a better future. It's about taking steps, big or small, toward that hope.

God has a plan for each and every one of us. He gives us unique talents and skills that can shape the world for the better. When we align our hopes with God's heart and connect to His source of infinite hope, He empowers us to fight for change and create a lasting impact.

Together, we can make the world a more colorful, delicious place to live. Keep shining your light and spreading hope everywhere you go!

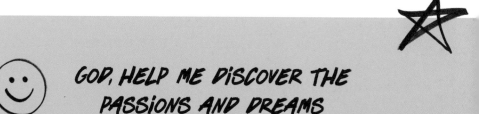

GOD, HELP ME DISCOVER THE PASSIONS AND DREAMS
YOU HAVE PLACED INSIDE ME, AND GUIDE ME IN MAKING CHOICES THAT HONOR YOUR CREATION AND BRING HOPE TO OTHERS. AMEN.

ONE TRILLION TREES

Trust in the Lord with all your heart, and do not
lean on your own understanding. In all your ways
acknowledge him, and he will make straight your paths.

PROVERBS 3:5–6 ESV

Have you ever had an idea that you thought might just change the world? Felix Finkbeiner did—and he was right.

Felix was just a regular kid like you, living in Germany. But one day, when he was only nine years old, he learned about the problem of deforestation, or cutting down entire forests of trees. You see, trees are super important to the health of the earth. Trees absorb carbon dioxide, a gas that is harmful to the environment in large amounts. Trees are important to the water cycle, acting as sponges by absorbing rainfall and releasing it slowly. They are homes to many animal species on the brink of extinction.

Felix not only learned just how important trees are but also heard about Wangari Maathai, a brave woman from Kenya who inspired people to plant over thirty million trees to help the environment. Moved by her story, Felix shared an idea with classmates, friends, and teachers.

They formed a team called Plant-for-the-Planet and set a goal to plant one million trees in every country. That's almost two hundred million trees worldwide! That's a whole lot of oxygen and shade, my friends.

They started organizing tree-planting events, where kids from different schools joined forces and got their hands dirty. They dug holes, planted saplings, and watered them with love and care. With every tree they planted, Felix and his team were making a difference, not just for the environment but also for the future.

Soon, other kids from around the world heard about Plant-for-the-Planet and wanted to join the movement. Kids were planting trees in countries far and wide! Can you imagine that? Though they were all from different cultures and spoke different languages, they were united by a common goal. And together, they planted millions and millions of trees!

Today, nearly one hundred thousand kids in seventy-five different countries have gotten involved in Plant-for-the-Planet. They teach one another about how to take care of the environment, plant trees, give speeches, protest, and so much more. Felix's idea and passion gained such a following that he had to set a new goal: planting one *trillion* trees worldwide. Now that's some big God-sized hope!

Just like Felix, God has a plan for each one of us. Sometimes the world's problems seem overwhelming, like a forest of challenges. But when we trust in the Lord with all our hearts and lean on His understanding, amazing things can happen.

So my friends, let's be inspired by Felix's story. Let's trust in God's guidance and take action fueled by hope for the future. Together, we can make this world a better place for everyone.

GOD, HELP ME HAVE FAITH

THAT I CAN MAKE A POSITIVE IMPACT IN THE WORLD AND THE COURAGE TO TAKE ACTION. GUIDE MY STEPS AND USE ME TO BRING HOPE AND CHANGE. AMEN.

REFRESHING GOALS

Wait for the Lord; be strong and take
heart and wait for the Lord.

PSALM 27:14 NIV

When I was a kid, I had my heart set on this supercool toy, but I couldn't afford it. So I decided to set up a lemonade stand in front of my house to earn some extra cash. I was determined to make my dream come true!

Years later in 2013, Vivienne Harr had the same idea as me. Only . . . she had her heart set on something BIG—much bigger than a supercool toy. She wanted to end child slavery all around the world.

Vivienne was eight years old when she learned about children who were forced to work long hours in factories instead of going to school and playing with friends. Fueled by the hope God puts in every one of us, she decided to make a difference. She set up a lemonade stand in a local park and sold cups of hope to raise money and bring attention to the issue of child slavery. Kids from all around came to her stand to support her mission. It was like a refreshing fiesta of compassion!

Vivienne didn't stop at one lemonade sale. She sold lemonade every single day! She wanted to raise $100,000 to give to organizations working to end child slavery. Then she had another idea.

Instead of charging a set price, she thought, *Why not let people pay what's in their hearts?* Vivienne changed the price of her lemonade to "FREE because every child should be free."

As word got out through social media, the average amount of money people donated for every cup of lemonade skyrocketed from $2 to $18! One person even paid $1,000 for a cup!

Five and a half months later, Vivienne reached her goal. But she still didn't stop! She continued to raise over $1 million and started a lemonade-bottling company. "Make a Stand" lemonade was sold in stores all over the country. With each bottle sold, Vivienne raised money to support organizations fighting against child slavery.

What cause are you most passionate about? What change do you hope to see in the future? When we connect to the hope found in God, we gain the courage to stand up for what's right, just like Vivienne did. We become unstoppable forces of change! So let's keep our eyes open and our hearts ready to make a stand.

Support animal welfare by volunteering at a local animal shelter. Make a difference in the fight against hunger by organizing a food drive. Help everyone access good education by organizing a book drive, collecting school supplies for kids who need them, or offering to tutor or mentor younger kids. Together, we can make this world a better place, one cup of hope at a time!

GOD, THANK YOU FOR SHOWING ME

THAT I CAN MAKE A DIFFERENCE WHEN I AM CONNECTED TO YOUR HOPE. HELP ME SEE THE HEARTBREAKING SITUATIONS AROUND ME, AND GIVE ME THE COURAGE TO TAKE ACTION THAT LEADS TO A BETTER FUTURE. AMEN.

A HOPEFUL COUNTDOWN

> As for you, be strong and do not give up,
> for your work will be rewarded.
> *2 CHRONICLES 15:7 NIV*

an you believe it? We've reached the final devotional on this journey of hope together. We've learned so much about the power of hope, how limitless hope comes only from God, and how it empowers us to make a difference in the world. This may be the last devotional of the book, but our hope journey is far from over. I want to share a special story that will remind us of something important as we continue to share God's limitless hope with the world.

A few years ago, I decided to put up this huge Christmas countdown sign in my front yard. It was cool and all, but . . . it ended up being a bigger hassle than I anticipated. You see, every single morning, in freezing cold weather, I had to trudge out there in my pajamas and physically change the number on the sign. It was a lot of work!

But here's the beautiful part of the story. One day, I found a note stuffed in my mailbox. It was from a little girl in my neighborhood named Ellen. She had drawn a picture of my home, complete with the Christmas countdown sign. And it hit me right in the heart. You know why? Because it made me realize that all the effort and time I put into that sign was worth it.

Sometimes we may not see the immediate results of our actions. We might wonder if the things we do to spread hope really make a difference. But they matter more than we could ever imagine. The encouragement you give your teacher, the smile that lights up your friend's face when they receive a note from you, or the moment you pray for someone right there on the spot—these seemingly small acts bring hope to others.

So my incredible amigos and amigas, though our journey is coming to an end, the hope we've found in God has only just begun. Keep shining your light throughout the world. ¡Adiós for now, but never goodbye!

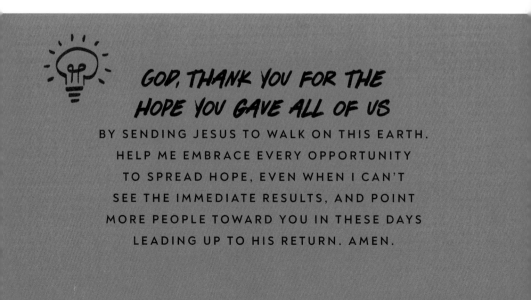

GOD, THANK YOU FOR THE HOPE YOU GAVE ALL OF US

BY SENDING JESUS TO WALK ON THIS EARTH.
HELP ME EMBRACE EVERY OPPORTUNITY
TO SPREAD HOPE, EVEN WHEN I CAN'T
SEE THE IMMEDIATE RESULTS, AND POINT
MORE PEOPLE TOWARD YOU IN THESE DAYS
LEADING UP TO HIS RETURN. AMEN.

ORGANIZATIONS THAT BRING HOPE

FREE WHEELCHAIR MISSION

You can help provide the gift of mobility to people living with disabilities around the world. One great way to get involved is by joining the Move for Mobility, which allows you to run, walk, hike, roll, swim, jump, bike, or do any other activity of your choice to raise funds for new wheelchairs.

https://www.freewheelchairmission.org/

AGAPE INTERNATIONAL MISSIONS (AIM)

Bring freedom to children living in modern-day slavery by partnering with AIM. Download their free prayer guide and begin a practice of asking God to rescue, heal, and protect these hurting children and to inspire others to take action.

https://www.aimfree.org/

HEARTS AGAINST HATE

Join the fight against discrimination toward people in the Asian American and Pacific Islander (AAPI) community. You can serve as an online volunteer for the organization or sign up to start your own Hearts Against Hate chapter, which will equip you to spread awareness, raise funds, and create care packages.

https://www.instagram.com/heartsagainsthate/

SAMARITAN'S PURSE: OPERATION CHRISTMAS CHILD

Send a special Christmas gift across the globe to a child in need. Start by decorating a shoebox your family isn't using, then get your parents to help you print a label and fill the box with medium and small gifts. Before you send your box, write a personal note of encouragement to the kid who will receive it.

https://www.samaritanspurse.org/what-we-do/
operation-christmas-child/

FILTER OF HOPE: KIDS' CLEAN WATER PROJECT

Participate in a free program that will teach you about the water-related needs of people around the world. As you watch the lessons, you'll also complete activities and learn how you can raise money for water filters—just ten dollars is enough to provide a child in need with water for ten years.

https://www.alltruists.com/

PLANT-FOR-THE-PLANET

This initiative empowers kids like you to fight the climate crisis. You can attend the online academy to become a Climate Justice Ambassador, organize a tree-planting event, create a little rainforest at home, and even start your own Plant-for-the-Planet Club.

https://www.plant-for-the-planet.org/

189

ABOUT THE AUTHOR AND ILLUSTRATOR

CARLOS WHITTAKER is a storyteller, speaker, and author of *Moment Maker, Kill the Spider,* and *Enter Wild,* as well as his latest release, *How to Human.* He frequently speaks at some of the nation's largest churches, corporations, and culture-shaping conferences with a superpower in creating spaces—online and in person—where people feel safe to engage in genuine dialogue and be themselves. Carlos is a People's Choice Award winner and host of the popular *Human Hope* podcast. He lives in Nashville with his wife, Heather, and their three children.

ARTHUR MOUNT is an artist based on the central California coast. His work appears regularly in national publications in the US and around the world. In addition to illustrating over fifty books, his work is also seen in advertising, broadcast, billboards, and coffee mugs. He received the D&AD Silver Pencil in 2005.

From the Publisher

GREAT BOOKS
ARE EVEN BETTER WHEN THEY'RE SHARED!

Help other readers find this one:

- Post a review at your favorite online bookseller

- Post a picture on a social media account and share why you enjoyed it

- Send a note to a friend who would also love it—or better yet, give them a copy

Thanks for reading!